IN

BEYOND ROME

T

ACI

ND

R

Pen & Sword
MILITARY

First published in Great Britain in 2018 by
PEN & SWORD MILITARY
An imprint of
Pen & Sword Books Ltd
47 Church Street
Barnsley
South Yorkshire
S70 2AS

ISBN 978-1-52672-709-1

Typeset by Concept, Huddersfield, West Yorkshire HD4 5JL.
Printed and bound in India by Replika Press Pvt. Ltd.

Pen & Sword Books Limited incorporates the imprints of Atlas, Archaeology, Aviation, Discovery, Family History, Fiction, History, Maritime, Military, Military Classics, Politics, Select, Transport, True Crime, Air World, Frontline Publishing, Leo Cooper, Remember When, Seaforth Publishing, The Praetorian Press, Wharncliffe Local History, Wharncliffe Transport, Wharncliffe True Crime and White Owl.

For a complete list of Pen & Sword titles please contact
PEN & SWORD BOOKS LIMITED
47 Church Street, Barnsley, South Yorkshire S70 2AS, England
E-mail: enquiries@pen-and-sword.co.uk
Website: www.pen-and-sword.co.uk

Contents

Acknowledgements

This archival photograph volume in the *Images of War* series is dedicated to the men and women who fought and perished in central and northern Italy during the summer and early autumn of 1944, extending well into 1945 to continue to drive the Nazis from the Italian mainland as the Allied armies moved towards the Alps. We ponder, upon viewing the photographs, about the heroic sacrifice made to maintain freedom lest we forget. The author also wishes to acknowledge the many military history scholars, past and present; including such names as Blumenson, Orgill, Fisher, Graham, Bidwell, D'Este, Ellis, Neillands, Strawson, Konstam, Zaloga, Ford, Clark, Atkinson and Whitlock, to name but a few, who have catalogued the nuances of this protracted campaign with their superlative prose. The author is indebted to the able assistance of the archivists at both the United States Army Military History Institute (USAMHI) at the United States Army War College in Carlisle, Pennsylvania, and the Still Photo Section of the National Archives and Records Administration (NARA) in College Park, Maryland.

Chapter One

Strategic Prelude to the Campaign Beyond Rome

few years before the Allied quest for Rome began, a series of 'see-saw' North African desert battles (the 'Benghazi Handicap'), spanning along an eastward-running axis of Beda Fomm-Benghazi-Tobruk-El Alamein along both the littoral of Libya's Cyrenaican province and Egypt's western frontier, occurred from December 1940 until August 1942. These numerous campaigns first pitted General Archibald Wavell, Commander-in-Chief, Middle East, and his Western Desert Force (later to become British XIII Corps under Lieutenant-General Richard O'Connor) against Axis forces, initially comprising the Italian Tenth Army, which was then buttressed by the *Deutsches Afrika Korps* (DAK) capably led by the renowned German commander, General (later Field Marshal) Erwin Rommel, until July 1941.

Then an expanding British and Commonwealth presence, to combat the now-designated Axis *Panzergruppe Afrika's* thrusts, was amalgamated into the British Eighth Army, led by a succession of commanders, until General Claude Auchinleck, the Commander-in-Chief, Middle East, took over the formation personally after the disastrous Gazala battles in May–June 1942, resulting in Tobruk's capitulation on 21 June. Auchinleck presided over the strategic but not tactical victory at the First Battle of El Alamein in July 1942, which halted Rommel's *Panzerarmee Afrika* (renamed in January 1942) advance on Alexandria. In a mid-August Cairo summit, prime minister Winston Churchill sacked Auchinleck, and Lieutenant-General Bernard Montgomery serendipitously took over the reins of Eighth Army, following the tragic death of British desert veteran XIII Corps commander, Lieutenant-General William 'Strafer' Gott. Under the command of the new Commander-in-Chief, Middle East, General Harold Alexander, Montgomery revitalised his Eighth Army. From 31 August to 4 September, Montgomery defeated Rommel's attack on the El Alamein Line during the Battle of Alam Halfa. Later, he won the decisive Second Battle of El Alamein in early November 1942 and then methodically pursued Rommel's German-Italian *Panzer-armee* back across Egypt's Western and the Libyan Deserts into south-eastern Tunisia by late January 1943. On 9 March, Rommel left Africa never to return.

Coincident with the British victory at the Second Battle of El Alamein was Operation Torch, the Anglo-American invasion of French north-west Africa at beaches near Casablanca, Oran and Algiers in Morocco, and Algeria. After the rapid capitulation of Vichy French forces there, six months of bloody Tunisian combat between the British First Army and US II Corps and a new Axis Army Groups Africa (*Heeresgruppe Afrika*) ensued with the ultimate surrender of Axis bridgeheads in Bizerte and Tunis in early May 1943.

With the supreme Allied commander, General Dwight Eisenhower, having amassed a large expeditionary force in North African ports, along with Churchill's zeal to 'knock' Italy out of the war and tie down German formations along Europe's 'soft underbelly', Sicily was invaded on 10 July 1943 during Operation Husky. The US Seventh and British Eighth armies, under lieutenant-generals George Patton and Montgomery, respectively, required thirty-eight days to force a tenacious Axis foe to evacuate the island to the Italian mainland across the Strait of Messina on 17 August. Benito Mussolini had been ousted as the fascist leader in late July, and on 8 September the Italian government capitulated precipitating a Nazi seizure of Italy. On 3 September, Eighth Army's British XIII Corps staged the uncontested Operation Baytown and seized many locales along the Calabrian toe of Italy, while elements of the British 1st Airborne Division amphibiously landed unopposed at Taranto, Operation Slapstick, along the peninsula's heel on 9 September.

On 9 September, a larger Allied amphibious assault landed Lieutenant-General Mark Clark's US Fifth Army, comprising British X and US VI Corps, along the beaches of the Gulf of Salerno to Naples' south. Initial attempts by only the German 16th Panzer Division failed to dislodge the Allies from their beachheads. However, within days, German Tenth Army commander, General Heinrich von Vietinghoff, amassed the XIV and LXXVI Panzer Corps and struck the Allied perimeter, almost compelling Clark's evacuation of the US VI Corps from the battlefield's southern end and resituating it in British X Corps' northern sector. On 18 September, Vietinghoff withdrew his Nazi divisions to a temporary defensive line along the Volturno River, north of Naples. The Allies entered the Neapolitan port on 1 October and began extensive repair of the German-demolished dock facilities.

German Field Marshal Albert Kesselring, commanding the Nazi forces in southern Italy, ordered Vietinghoff to hold the Volturno River line until 15 October, enabling the completion of the more-temporary Barbara and Bernhardt Lines, while more substantive fortifications were erected on the Gustav Line, which ran along the Garigliano and Rapido rivers, stretching from the Tyrrhenian Sea in the west to north of the Sangro River's mouth on the Adriatic coast in the east.

While Montgomery's Eighth Army units battled to the east of the Apennine Mountain spine at such locales as Fossacesia, Mozzogrogna, Orsogna and Ortona, Clark's Fifth Army campaigned in a wet, cold climate amid the massif comprising the pillars of the Mignano Gap, in an attempt to gain entry into the Liri Valley to the south of Cassino and then 'onto Rome'. After Clark's disastrous attempt to cross the Rapido River in front of Cassino, with two regiments of his US 36th Division, ended in failure on 20–22 January 1944, his other US II Corps-reinforced 34th Division along with the French Expeditionary Corps (FEC), the latter under the capable French general, Alphonse Juin, almost seized the Benedictine abbey and Monte Cassino during the early days of February. However, their attacks faltered amid a determined Nazi resistance and Allied exhaustion, as the recently formed II New Zealand Corps under General Bernard Freyberg, comprising the 2nd New Zealand and 4th Indian divisions, was held in reserve rather than committed to the tail-end of the hard-pressed Allied mountain attack north of the town. The First Battle of Cassino ended with the Germans in possession of the town, the heights and the monastery looming above.

A three-month-long stalemate developed along the Nazi defensive Gustav Line to the south of Rome, notably at the town of Cassino, which governed the entrance into the Liri Valley and the pathway to the Italian capital. Winston Churchill desperately wanted to quickly capture the Eternal City as an Axis capital, even after Italy's capitulation and transition to an Allied co-belligerent status. However, deadly combat was to pervade during the Second and Third battles for Cassino in February and March, respectively, as well as at a US VI Corps beachhead at Anzio that was initially established unopposed on 22 January, 30 miles to the south of Rome. The Allied Operation Shingle at Anzio to bypass the Gustav Line and become an accelerated pathway to Rome was instead quickly contained and then besieged by the German Fourteenth Army under General Eberhard von Mackensen.

During mid-May 1944, the formidable Gustav Line was pierced by the Allied Fifth and Eighth armies under the leadership of 15th Army Group commander General Harold Alexander. During the last week of May, the US VI Corps broke out from its beleaguered Anzio bridgehead as British XIII and I Canadian Corps drove through the Liri Valley onward to Rome. After a controversial alteration in plans, some of Clark's American divisions captured Valmontone while other British and American forces broke the German Fourteenth Army's Caesar Line. The Eternal City was declared an open one by the Nazis on 3 July, and American elements of Clark's Fifth Army triumphantly entered the city on 5 June, a day before the momentous Allied Normandy invasion.

(**Above**) British soldiers load supplies into a truck at a Benghazi, Libya dock in early February 1941 for transport to British XIII Corps frontlines after their lightning offensive (Operation Compass) against the Italian Tenth Army that commenced in early December 1940 and ended with the destruction of this Axis formation at Beda Fomm on 7 February. A series of 'see-saw' campaigns (the 'Benghazi Handicap') pitted Wavell's British XIII Corps against Axis forces commanded by Rommel, who arrived in Tripoli on 12 February, to form the nidus of his vaunted DAK) in the Cyrenaican third of Libya and Egypt's western desert from late February to June 1941. After Auchinleck succeeded Wavell as Commander-in-Chief, Middle East, a steady stream of reinforcements allowed the Allied desert formations to become British Eighth Army on 1 November 1941, under Lieutenant-General Alan Cunningham. (NARA)

(**Opposite, above**) A British Eighth Army truck carries Free French soldiers kitted in British equipment to the Gazala Line in late May 1942. After horrific armour and infantry combat, the Free French position at Bir Hacheim was overrun and captured on 10 June while other Eighth Army fixed positions, under Lieutenant-General Neil Ritchie, were also vanquished by Rommel's now *Panzerarmee Afrika*, leading to the fall of Tobruk on 21 June and the awarding of a field marshal's baton. (NARA)

(**Opposite, below**) A column of British M4 medium tanks pursues fleeing Axis units of the now named German-Italian *Panzerarmee* in mid-November 1942 after Montgomery's Eighth Army victory at the Second Battle of El Alamein (23 October–4 November). The Axis forces were to continue their retreat across the Egyptian frontier and throughout the entire Libyan littoral into south-eastern Tunisia by the end of January 1943. (NARA)

A Vichy French gun battery at Safi on the Atlantic coast of Morocco as Patton's western task force made amphibious landings on 8 November 1942 during Operation Torch hazardous for the Allies. After overcoming Vichy French resistance throughout Morocco and Algeria, the strategic ports of Casablanca, Oran and Algiers were captured by the Allies for their offensive into Tunisia. (*USAMHI*)

British First Army infantrymen, under Lieutenant-General Kenneth Anderson, are escorted by US II Corps M3 light tanks during their December offensive into Tunisia (the 'Race for Tunis') after the successful earlier Torch landings. However, the German and Italian forces reacted more quickly, with Hitler creating bridgeheads at Tunis and Bizerte for a new 5th *Panzerarmee*, under General Hans-Jürgen von Arnim, turning the Tunisian campaign into a brutal six-month ordeal. (*NARA*)

British Eighth Army infantrymen of the 1st Armoured Division's 7th Rifle Brigade crouch in the tall vegetation of the Kounine Hills near Sousse in north-eastern Tunisia before advancing on an Axis position in early May 1943. After pursuing Rommel's German-Italian *Panzerarmee* into Tunisia and piercing the Mareth Line in late March, Montgomery's Eighth Army closed up on Sousse and then Enfidaville, leaving the capture of Tunis to British First Army's V and IX Corps and Bizerte to US II Corps. (*NARA*)

A Gurkha infantryman from Eighth Army's 4th Indian Division, which had been in combat on the African continent since December 1940, brandishes his honed *kukri* knife to celebrating Tunisians on 10 May 1943. All of north Africa was cleared of the Axis with a massive surrender, dubbed 'Tunisgrad'. (*NARA*)

(**Above**) Patton, commanding general of the US Seventh Army, steps off of an American landing craft onto the dock at the southern Sicilian port of Licata. The US 3rd Infantry Division, under Major-General Lucian Truscott, landed successfully there against light opposition, with the support of elements of the US 2nd Armoured Division, on 10 July 1943. A Patton-initiated reconnaissance-in-force with a Provisional Corps, headed by his Seventh Army deputy, Major-General Geoffrey Keyes, was approved by Alexander on 17 July. Five days later, the island's capital of Palermo on the northern coast was captured. (*NARA*)

(**Opposite, above**) Canadian 1st Division infantrymen march along a road, passing an M4 medium tank of the Canadian 1st Armoured Brigade, from Valguarnera towards Enna in late July 1943. The Canadians were part of British XXX Corps' Sicilian offensive, Operation Hardgate, moving along a west-to-east axis past Enna and Leonforte and onto Regalbuto. Hardgate's objective, along with XXX Corps' 78th Infantry Division, was to capture Adrano, a major road junction on the south-western side of the Italian massif, Mount Etna. (*NARA*)

(**Opposite, below**) Infantrymen from the British XXX Corps' 78th Division lead their pack mule in the vicinity of Bronte on their trek towards Randazzo during the second week of August 1943. Randazzo, like Adrano, was a key Sicilian road junction on the northern side of Mount Etna, where infantry regiments of the US 1st Division met their British counterparts. (*NARA*)

The main signatories of an Italian armistice meet on 3 September 1943 in secret to execute the document. From left-to-right are: Major-General Walter Bedell Smith (*seated*), General Eisenhower's chief of staff; Commodore Reyer Mylions Dick, Royal Navy; Major-General Lowell Rocks, US Army; Captain de Hand, an *aide-de-camp* to Brigadier Kenneth Strong, British Army and Eisenhower's chief intelligence officer (*standing to the right*); Italian Lieutenant-General Aldo Castilland (in mufti); Mr Montenari, an emissary from the Italian Foreign Ministry (*far right*). The armistice was officially announced on 8 September, a day before the amphibious assault along the beaches in the Gulf of Salerno by Clark's US Fifth Army. (*NARA*)

The deposed Italian fascist dictator Benito Mussolini with German glidermen who rescued him in the Gran Sasso raid on 12 September 1943 at Campo Imperatore in the Abruzzi Apennines. Earlier on 24 July, Rome's fascist grand council voted against Mussolini's stay in power, which was affirmed by the Italian King, Victor Emmanuel, the next day. After his rescue, Mussolini was made leader of the Italian Social Republic, a German puppet state in Nazi-occupied Italy. (*Author's Collection*)

British sappers use magnetic mine detectors along the beaches of Reggio di Calabria after their unopposed amphibious assault across the Strait of Messina to the Italian mainland on 3 September 1943. The combination of German rear-guard action, poor roads, Nazi demolitions and booby traps, and a shortage of Eighth Army motor transport nullified Montgomery's forces from participating in the critical action along the beaches in the Gulf of Salerno. (NARA)

Royal Army Medical Corps personnel attached to British X Corps of the US Fifth Army participate in a burial detail along the northern beaches of the Allied perimeter at Salerno in mid-September 1943. Both American and British sectors were besieged by fierce German Tenth Army armoured counter-attacks. At one point, fearing a breakthrough to the sea, Clark, the Fifth Army commander, briefly contemplated evacuating his US VI Corps' 36th and 45th Infantry divisions into the British X Corps zone, but his Allied subordinate commanders protested vehemently as the crisis began to wane. (NARA)

(**Above**) US Fifth Army soldiers man a captured German 20mm *Flakvierling* (Flak) 38 quadruple-barrelled anti-aircraft (AA) gun at Paestum on 15 September 1943. This weapon was introduced by the Germans in 1940 and the four barrels was the most expedient method of compensating for the lack of knockdown capability in the single-barrelled AA gun. The *Luftwaffe* launched repeated fighter, fighter-bomber, bomber and guided pilotless bomb attacks against Allied offshore shipping, inflicting heavy losses on the US and Royal navies. (*USAMHI*).

(**Opposite, above**) US VI Corps infantrymen pull the rope of a hastily constructed ferry to bring their assault boat across the rain-swollen Volturno River, which was an excellent temporary defensive water obstacle for the Nazis north of Naples, in October 1943. The river rises in the mountains near Isernia in the US VI Corps' sector and is conjoined by the waters of the Calore River. This meandering river with numerous turns then flows towards Castel Volturno on the Tyrrhenian coast, through such locales as Capua and Grazzanise, which were to be assault points for the British X Corps' 56th Infantry and 7th Armoured divisions, respectively. (*NARA*)

(**Opposite, below**) A Canadian 1st Infantry Division patrol runs cautiously along a road with the snow-covered Apennine Mountains in the background. To Rome's south, the Apennines formed a mountainous spine down the Italian Peninsula. The Canadians, part of Lieutenant-General Miles Dempsey's British XIII Corps, fought through the mountains on a north-eastern vector towards the Sangro and Moro rivers to the Adriatic Sea port of Ortona. (*NARA*)

A Canadian M4 medium tank crewman and accompanying Canadian 1st Division infantrymen advance through the ruins of Ortona at the end of December 1943. The approach to Ortona had been difficult for the Canadians as they had to cross the Moro River and nearby ridges, all defended by elements of the German 90th Panzer Grenadier, 26th Panzer and 1st Parachute divisions. Within Ortona, the Nazi parachutists fought with suicidal tenacity necessitating a house-to-house struggle with infantry, armour and 6-pounder anti-tank (AT) artillery pieces, all needed to reduce enemy bunkers and machine-gun positions. (NARA)

A Canadian 1st Division infantryman inspects a German fortified machine-gun position in Ortona at the end of December 1943. Five days of combat were required for the Canadians to capture the port city. After the action, the Canadians were recognised as being expert in urban combat tactics against a determined bunkered enemy. *(NARA)*

Three members from a Royal Army Medical Corps team administer plasma intravenously to a wounded British X Corps soldier on the Garigliano River front in mid-January 1944. As part of the US Fifth Army's winter offensive against the Gustav Line, Lieutenant-General Richard McCreery's British X Corps infantry divisions; the 5th, 56th and 46th, assaulting across the river had achieved only mixed results in the sector from the Tyrrhenian coast north to the village of Sant Ambroglio, just south of the Liri River and Valley. *(NARA)*

(**Above**) Two British X Corps infantrymen scurry among the buildings in an Italian village during attempts to breach the Gustav Line across the Garigliano River well to the south of the Liri Valley during the First Battle for Cassino in mid-January 1944. McCreery's forces met fierce resistance from the German 94th Panzer Grenadier Division's defenders north of Minturno and in the Montes Maio-Juga massif on the western side of the river. (*NARA*)

(**Opposite, above**) Part of a British X Corps infantry section is shown along the Garigliano River front in mid-January 1944. Two of the three infantrymen are armed with Thompson 0.45-inch calibre submachine-guns, while the middle one is about to hurl a Mills bomb at enemy positions. The German defenders were well entrenched in the Gustav Line's fortified positions that had taken months to complete by Todt Organisation engineers and conscripted Italian labourers. (*NARA*)

(**Opposite, below**) An American M7 105mm Gun Motor Carriage (GMC) or 'Priest' is shown under a camouflage net with its front end elevated on rocks to augment the trajectory arc of its shell fired in support of the infantrymen of the US 36th Division's 141st and 143rd regiments attempting to cross the Rapido River south of Cassino on 20–22 January 1944. These valiant efforts of part of Major-General Keyes' US II Corps turned into a suicidal disaster against fortified positions along the Gustav Line at locales such as Sant Angelo and Pignataro in the Liri Valley. (*NARA*)

A US II Corps infantryman in the 34th Division loads ammunition onto the carrier of his pack mule in the mountainous terrain to the north of Cassino during an attack that began on 20 January and extended until the first week of February 1944. The US 133rd, 135th, 168th Infantry regiments of the 34th Division, along with the attached 142nd Infantry Regiment from the 36th Division (having not participated in the Rapido River assault) successfully crossed the Rapido north of Cassino and after prolonged mountain combat, came to within 1,000 yards of the abbey's walls before becoming exhausted as well as short of manpower and ammunition. In a controversial move, the British Eighth Army's 2nd New Zealand Division, which was sent to relieve the US 34th Division, was not utilised in this attack. Lieutenant-General Bernard Freyberg's troops, along with Major-General Francis Tuker's 4th Indian Division, were to subsequently attack both the town and Benedictine monastery during the Second and Third Battles for Cassino in unsuccessful assaults in February and March 1944. (*USAMHI*)

(**Opposite, above**) The crew of an American 57mm AT gun prepares for an anticipated German counter-attack after the failed US 36th Infantry Division's Rapido River assault on 20–22 January 1944. The snow-capped Monte Cairo (*far background*) towers over Monte Cassino below with its Benedictine abbey situated on top. (*USAMHI*)

(**Opposite, below**) French Expeditionary Corps (FEC) soldiers in the US Fifth Army pass a destroyed Nazi MkIV Panzer north of Cassino during their late January/early February 1944 attack. These troops were from the Moroccan 2nd and Algerian 3rd Infantry divisions and, as many were tribesmen from the Maghreb, they possessed tremendous mountain warfare skills and *élan*. These infantry divisions successfully crossed the Rapido to the north of the US 34th Division between Sant Elia and Monte Santa Croce and captured some heights within the Monte Cairo massif, such as at Colle Belvedere and cut the road to Atina in the north. (*NARA*)

(**Opposite, above**) US VI Corps infantrymen from Major-General Lucian Truscott's 3rd Division wade ashore unopposed after descending the ramps of a Landing Craft Infantry (LCI) transport along the beaches to the east of Anzio Harbour during Operation Shingle on 22 January 1944. Major-General John Lucas's VI Corps' 'end-run' had caught the Germans by surprise. Rather than pressing forward to the Alban Hills and, perhaps, north to Rome, Lucas consolidated his beachhead for the next eight days, allowing the German Fourteenth Army's divisions to concentrate and contain the Allied perimeter. (*NARA*)

(**Opposite, below**) A British 1st Division M7 105mm GMC or 'Priest' leads the way for a column of trucks disembarking from an Allied Landing Ship Tank (LST) of Task Force Peter over a pontoon bridge to the north of Anzio as part of the US VI Corps' uncontested amphibious landings on 22 January 1944. Due to an unfavourable hydrographic gradient, some of the British landing forces had to be moved to the American sector of the beachhead at Anzio Harbour. (*NARA*)

(**Above**) British-crewed Amphibious DUKWs ride out of the surf onto the beaches at Anzio to bring needed supplies to sustain the beachhead's perimeter after the unopposed landings of 22 January 1944. German General Eberhard von Mackensen had successfully ringed the Allied perimeter with his Fourteenth Army divisions and, in early February, commenced a series of savage counter-attacks against the US VI Corps forces which, in essence, created a siege-like state. (*USAMHI*)

Two US VI Corps signalmen work in underground headquarters' cellars below the surface of Nettuno to arrange the communications wires with the various commands and rear echelon. Nazi aerial and artillery bombardment were capable of penetrating a few dozen feet of subterranean earth and masonry structures. (*USAMHI*)

(**Opposite, above**) American and British soldiers share a bivouac area within the surrounded Anzio beachhead. The Allied perimeter was isolated by land from the US Fifth Army and was supplied solely by seaborne reinforcement from Naples under the threat of ubiquitous *Luftwaffe* aerial anti-shipping attacks. In addition to the Nazi Panzer-infantry counter-attacks of early February 1944, the beachhead was also subjected to German artillery shelling from the Alban Hills and beyond. (*USAMHI*)

(**Opposite, below**) In Anzio Harbour during the siege, two American soldiers are shown manning a 40mm Bofors AA gun during a lull in the *Luftwaffe* aerial assault as others are seen loading supplies onto trucks for distribution to Allied forces in the perimeter. The German Fourteenth Army commanding general, Mackensen, wanted the Allied transport and cargo ships offshore attacked as these vessels were sustaining the US VI Corps bridgehead despite his violent and costly counter-attacks. (*USAMHI*)

(**Above**) A Maori infantryman from the 28th Battalion of the 5th New Zealand Brigade guards German prisoners captured during the Second Battle for Cassino on 17 February 1944. The Maoris crossed the Rapido-flooded terrain from the east along a narrow railway causeway and captured Cassino's railway station and German soldiers. However, despite a masking smokescreen to protect the New Zealand sappers from German gunfire while erecting Bailey bridges for Allied armour and AT guns, Nazi shelling prevented the Maoris' reinforcement, necessitating their withdrawal when their ammunition was exhausted. Over 125 Maoris were killed or wounded. (*NARA*)

(**Opposite, above**) A trio of New Zealand artillery spotters observe the effects of Allied aerial and artillery bombardment on the town of Cassino (*white smoke below the heights*) and Castle Hill, from where black plumes of smoke emanated on 15 March 1944. Atop Monte Cassino (*left of Castle Hill*), the remains of the Benedictine abbey from the February aerial bombardment were visible. To the left of Monte Cassino was Highway 6, the entrance into the Liri Valley, which had evaded Allied capture for four months. (*NARA*)

(**Opposite, below**) A sniper of one of the 25th New Zealand Battalion's advancing companies amid the ruins of Cassino during the Third Battle for Cassino in mid-March 1944. Freyberg, commanding general of the II New Zealand Corps, had ordered a massive preliminary aerial bombardment of the town of Cassino, which demolished all the remaining standing structures turning the roads into a rubble-strewn moonscape. Despite Castle Hill being captured by some New Zealand infantry units, large bomb craters prohibited Allied armour movement through the town to seize the Nazi parachutist-occupied hotels Continental and des Roses, as well as other well-defended heights leading up to the abbey upon Monastery Hill. (*NARA*)

(**Above**) A destroyed M4 medium tank from B Squadron of the 19th New Zealand Armoured Brigade amid Cassino's ruins on 17 March 1944. Despite the presence of armoured support for the infantry, the town's cratered roads and masonry debris limited tactical co-operation and prevented the New Zealand infantry from reaching their targets in the town's centre. (*USAMHI*)

(**Opposite, above**) General Harold Alexander (*second from left*), Allied 15th Army group commander, speaks with war correspondents in Nettuno on 3 March 1944. Truscott (*far left*) had assumed command of US VI Corps in the Anzio perimeter on 23 February 1944 following the relief of Lucas. Alexander, along with his chief of staff, Lieutenant-General John Harding, had both reached the conclusion that a broad frontal assault utilising the numerous corps of Fifth and Eighth armies at Cassino and south to the Tyrrhenian coast was required to break the Gustav Line after the failed initial three battles to gain access to the Liri Valley. This decision evolved into Operation Diadem, which was to be unleashed on 11 May 1944. (*USAMHI*)

(**Opposite, below**) A heavily armed M3 half-track, with chains on the front wheels to traverse the muddy ground along the Tyrrhenian coast, is loaded with US Combat Engineers. At the southern end of the Gustav Line, the US II Corps' 85th and 88th Infantry divisions attacked inland from the Gulf of Gaeta from Tufo towards San Maria Infante and from south of Minturno along Highway 7 on the coast towards Formia on 11 May 1944. The American assault stalled, notably at San Maria Infante. (*NARA*)

(**Above**) An FEC pack mule train advances up the mountainous terrain of the Montes Maio-Faito massif to the north of Castelforte as part of Operation Diadem on 11 May 1944. The FEC's two infantry, one mountain and one motorised division, broke the Gustav Line within twenty-four hours at multiple sites. Capitalising on their breakthroughs, the FEC forces fanned out towards the foothills of the Aurunci Mountains, Ausonia, San Andrea, Sant Ambrogio and Sant Apollinaire by 13–14 May, sweeping behind the German lines towards the Liri Valley. By 15 May, the Germans withdrew from this area to avoid encirclement, which facilitated the stalled US II Corps' offensive. (USAMHI)

(**Opposite, above**) Universal Carriers of the Indian 8th Division of British XIII Corps prepare for their offensive across the Rapido River as part of Operation Diadem on 11 May 1944. Just south of Cassino and at Sant Angelo, British 4th and Indian 8th Indian divisions, respectively, gained small bridgeheads across the river. However, sluggish reinforcement resulting from delayed construction of armour and truck-supporting temporary bridges limited a breakout into the Liri Valley. (NARA)

(**Opposite, below**) British infantrymen of XIII Corps move through the ruins of Sant Angelo on 17 May after the British 78th Infantry Division, three days earlier, had passed through the Indian 8th Division's heavily contested bridgehead on the far side of the Rapido River and advanced on Pignataro. The British 78th Division now threatened a XIII Corps envelopment of Cassino's Nazi defenders, thereby prompting their retreat from the town and abbey on the night of 17 May. (NARA)

(**Above**) Infantrymen from the British 4th Division move into the ruins of Cassino from south of the town on 18 May 1944 after the Germans fled during the night before. The heavily contested Castle Hill looms in the background, which New Zealand infantrymen captured in mid-March during the opening of the Third Battle for Cassino. (*NARA*)

(**Opposite, above**) An M4 medium tank of the I Canadian Corps' 5th Armoured Division races up the road towards Sant Angelo while leaving a cloud of dust after the British XIII Corps breakthrough into the Liri Valley in mid-May 1944. The 1st Canadian Infantry Division, with its armoured support, was to now advance up the Liri Valley towards the Hitler Line, with British XIII Corps' divisions as its right flank. (*NARA*)

(**Opposite, below**) Canadian armoured cars move through Pontecorvo in late May 1944. After probing Nazi defences upon entering the Liri Valley, the I Canadian Corps attacked and broke through the Hitler Line of defences in the valley at Pontecorvo on 23 May and then continued onto Frosinone on 31 May on Highway 6, with British XIII Corps on their right flank attacking Aquino. (*NARA*)

(**Opposite, above**) On 23 May 1944, Operation Buffalo, Anzio's breakout commenced. Here, M4 medium tanks of the 1st Armoured Division, along with motorised infantry from the 6th Armoured Infantry Regiment, move forward along a muddy lane past their protective smokescreen (*background*). The primary target for Operation Buffalo was to pierce the German Fourteenth Army lines near Cisterna. (*NARA*)

(**Opposite, below**) A British Jeep passes a German corpse on the roadside near the dead artilleryman's wrecked field-gun at Anzio perimeter's western end. After an initial feint, the British 1st Division attacked northward astride the Via Anziate, while the British 5th Division crossed the Moletta River and advanced onto Ardea inland from the Tyrrhenian coast. The German Fourteenth Army resisted the Allied advance from the centre of the bridgehead along the Via Anziate from behind its Caesar Line fortifications that blocked the southern approaches to Rome along the Alban Hills' lowlands astride Highway 7. Although Mackensen enabled the remnants of his Fourteenth Army to safely withdraw across the Tiber River on 2 June 1944, he was relieved by Kesselring on 4 June. (*NARA*)

(**Above**) Infantrymen from the US Fifth Army wait along a road on the outskirts of Rome on 4 June 1944 for orders to advance further into the city's centre. German Field Marshal Kesselring had only days before requested from Berlin that Rome be designated an open city. Apart from limited Nazi rear-guard actions and demolitions, Clark's troops were poised for their triumphant entry into the Eternal City. (*USAMHI*)

A column of M10 tank destroyers proceeds towards the Roman Coliseum (*background*) along a street lined with the city's inhabitants on 5 June 1944. It had been almost eleven months since the invasion of Sicily and the Allied plan to knock Italy out of the war as a belligerent and seize the Axis junior partner's capital had come to fruition. Ironically, Clark's entry into Rome and the accompanying limelight were short-lived as the Allied landings along the Cotentin Peninsula in Normandy occurred the very next day. (*USAMHI*)

Chapter Two

Terrain, Fortifications and Weapons

Prominent terrain features

Although the Apennine Mountains between Rome and Bologna are specifically named for the Italian province or provinces in which they are located (i.e. Ligurian, Tuscan-Emilian, and Umbrian), it is also commonly referred to as the Northern Apennines. The Northern Apennines, containing peaks to above 7,000 feet, form an unbroken terrain barrier up to 50 miles deep and 140 miles long, stretching diagonally from north-west to south-east across the upper part of the Italian Peninsula from the Ligurian to the Adriatic Sea, before turning more southerly to become the country's spine. Coastal strips are situated along both western and eastern sides of the Northern Apennines.

The Romagna Plain of the Emilia Romagna region consists of a wide plain south of the Po River and a more mountainous area near the border of Monte Cimone, the highest peak in the Northern Apennines in Modena province. The area historically called Emilia is to the west and includes the provinces of Placenza, Parma, Reggio, Emilia, Modena, Ferrara and the western part of the province of Bologna. The area to the east, containing the provinces of Ravenna, Rimini, Forli and Cesena, is called Romagna. Within Emilia Romagna is also the independent Republic of San Marino, the most ancient republic in Europe.

Highway 9 (Via Emilia) runs north-west from Rimini on the Adriatic coast through the Romagna Plain to Bologna and then on to Modena and Placenza. The Eighth Army's advance from Rimini along the Adriatic coast through the towns and cities along Highway 9 on the Romagna Plain – Sant Arcangelo di Romagna, Cesena, Forli, Faenza and Imola – were to be heavily contested by the Nazis after the Gothic Line was pierced in early September 1944.

On the Adriatic coast, the Northern Apennines descend to become a line of ridges, ideal for defence, along the Romagna Plain. The Gemmano and Coriano ridges were tactically important features that dominated the coastline and approaches to Rimini by land. Here, the Romagna Plain consists of a series of hills and ridges across rain-soaked valleys just north of the Gothic Line. Fields with broken banks of streams and swamp-like ditches characterised this sector, which had once been marshland. In 1944–45, with drainage ditches destroyed and the river banks breached, the Romagna Plain was mostly flooded, not very suitable for armour. It was to become an Eighth Army's infantryman's nightmare.

Highway 16 is a north-westwardly-directed road running from the port of Rimini inland through Ravenna. This highway runs to the south of Lake Comacchio, an inland lake near the Adriatic coast, to Ravenna, before moving north-westward to Ferrara, just south of the Po River. Highway 16 provided excellent interior lines for Kesselring regarding supply and reinforcement in the Po Valley.

For any Eighth Army offensive in the spring of 1945, it would have to contend with the topography of Lake Comacchio, which interfered with any northerly advance along the Adriatic coast. Also in this sector are a series of rivers (from south to north): the Marecchia; the Fontanaccia; the Uso; and the Fiumicino, which run parallel to one another from their mountain sources south of Cesena and empty into the Adriatic coast north of Rimini. From 17 September to 1 October 1944, a series of hard-fought river crossings – the Battle of the Rivers – was to occur as the Eighth Army's *corps de chasse*, the 2nd New Zealand Division, attempted to advance northward against the retreating Nazis paralleling the Adriatic coast and its railway to Ravenna.

Additionally, to the north of Florence were other Northern Apennine mountain-derived rivers (from east to west) including the Savio, Ronco, Montone, Lamone, Senio, Santerno, Sillaro and Idice. Some of these rivers flow north toward the Po Valley, but then turn east towards the Adriatic Sea to link up with the circuitous Reno. The Reno River originates in the mountains south-west of Bologna and runs in a wide northerly arc past this major Emilia Romagna city for 30 miles towards Cento before turning south-east, parallel with the Po River to the north, until it joins the Senio near the southern shore of Lake Comacchio before emptying into the Adriatic.

For the Eighth Army to break out from the Romagna Plain to get to Bologna and into the Po Valley, these parallel rivers running north-eastward across Highway 9 and towards Lake Comacchio and the Adriatic had to be crossed. All were to serve as fall-back Nazi defence lines, each one possessing massive flood-bank ramparts. Two of the rivers, the Sillaro and the Idice, join up with the Reno near the towns of Argenta and Bastia. Argenta provided a dry gap between the flooded Nazi defence positions, which the German engineers had created by opening up some flood banks, adding to the naturally wet marshes along the southern shore of Lake Comacchio.

In Alexander's planning, if the Eighth Army captured Argenta during the spring 1945 offensive, then his British and Commonwealth divisions would outflank the Sillaro, the Idice and the Reno rivers. By so doing, the hinge of the German defensive system along the Romagna Plain would be destroyed and the way through the Po Valley to the Po River would be open. The terrain between the Reno and Po rivers was free of water obstacles, thus good tank country.

Another aspect of Alexander's strategy was for Clark's Fifth Army to proceed north through the mountains and cut Highway 9, which would imperil Kesselring's divisions for resupply and reinforcement on the Adriatic front. There are two major passes through the Northern Apennines to the north of Florence. The Futa Pass is 20 miles from Florence on Highway 65 and leads to Bologna. The Futa Pass defences were formidable with barbed wire, dug-in tank turrets, and a 3-mile anti-tank ditch. Approximately 7 miles to the east of the Futa Pass is the Il Giogo Pass that leads to Firenzuola, on secondary road No. 6528, which then runs to Imola on Highway 9. This pass was dominated on either side by Monticelli Ridge to the west and Monte Altuzzo to the east.

Both Allied armies campaigned to get into the Po Valley, which parallels the river and runs in an east-west direction. The Northern Apennines protected Bologna and an Allied entry into the Po Valley. The Germans built their fortifications at the Gothic Line and further north on mountains and ridgelines that provided optimal visualisation and fields of fire. As the mountainous ridges widened as they approached the Po Valley, trees, hedgerows and dykes provided the enemy with excellent cover.

The Po River originated in north-western Italy and moved east to empty into the Adriatic Sea at the Po Delta. The Po River is between 130–500 yards wide and was bordered by flood banks serving as obstacles in addition to the enemy field works along the river. The villages along the river also provided excellent masonry fortifications and observation points. The Allies destroyed the score of bridges spanning the Po River from Piacenza to the Adriatic coast to both interrupt Kesselring from getting reinforcements as well as cut off an orderly withdrawal of troops and ordnance to the northern bank of the river.

Fortification belts
Albert Line
The German Albert Line of defences ran east-to-west just to the north of Perugia in the foothills of the Apennines and to the west of the Tiber River. The Tiber River, one of the longest in Italy, rises in the Northern Apennines and flows southerly through the Umbria region to join the Aniene River and empty into the Tyrrhenian Sea south-west of Rome. Either side of Lake Trasimeno, in the centre of the weak fortification belt, was defended by the LXXVI Panzer Corps of the German Tenth Army. To the west of the LXXVI Panzer Corps was the left flank of the German Fourteenth Army. When the Nazi units retreating from the vicinity of Rome reached the Albert Line between 20–23 June 1944, the threat of Army Groups C's division and defeat in detail was averted. The Albert Line provided Kesselring with a site to re-join his Fourteenth and Tenth armies, withdrawing separately to the west of the Abruzzi Apennines.

Arno Line

The Arno Line was a makeshift German defensive belt centred on Florence and extended westward to the Tyrrhenian coast near Pisa and eastward to Bibbiena in the Northern Apennines. It was the final obstacle for the Fifth Army to encounter before contending with the Gothic Line, the last major defensive belt in northern Italy.

Gothic Line

The Gothic Line ran for approximately 200 miles through mostly depopulated areas from between Viareggio and La Spezia on Italy's western coast to the Foglia River valley near the Adriatic Sea's coastal heights between Pesaro to the south and Cattolica to the north. The belt's fortifications exploited the rugged Northern Apennines mountain passes, such as at the Futa and Il Giogo ones, north of Florence on the Arno River. Rommel surveyed this terrain in the fall of 1943 prior to his transfer to France and favourably rated it for a defensive zone. During the summer of 1944, the Todt Organisation's engineers comprising 2,000 Slovak technicians and 15,000 conscripted Italian labourers feverishly worked to complete this fortification line by the fall of 1944.

The Gothic Line plans utilised more than thirty steel- or concrete-mounted 75 or 88mm tank turrets (i.e. *Panzerturm*). Steel shelters, minefields, rock-carved fortified positions, miles of barbed wire and wide AT ditches were built. By the end of August, when the Allied attack commenced, there were more than 2,000 machine-gun positions, more than 450 AT guns, along with mortar and assault gun weapon pits. Almost all of the houses had been levelled with trees felled to establish machine-gun killing fields between approaches sown with landmines. Kesselring believed the Adriatic sector was especially strong as the defences had incorporated the foot-hills and ridges of the descending Northern Apennines, among which were situated the numerous intertwining rivers that the Allies had to cross. The Gothic Line, the Romagna Plain and the fortified Northern Apennines were the last main obstacles for the Allies south of the Po River and before the Alps. The same German Tenth and Fourteenth armies that had defied the Allied advance since September 1943 were now situated behind a strong fortification belt a year later.

Adige Line

In northern Italy, in addition to the Po River, were the Adige, the Brenta and the Piave rivers, which the Nazis planned to use as delaying terrain features. Of these, the Adige River was the most heavily fortified terrain line since it was backed by the Euganean Hills. The Adige Line was located in the Alpine foothills and ran east and west of Lake Garda. The fortifications; containing trenches, dug-outs, and machine-gun emplacements, resembled those from the First World War. They were designed to cover a final withdrawal of Nazi forces into north-east Italy and/or Austria.

Allied Tank-Infantry co-operation

In 1939, the standard British armoured division had six tank regiments to two infantry battalions. A year later, each tank brigade was allotted another motorised battalion, bringing the infantry formations to three. In 1941 and throughout the remainder of the war, there was a further modification of armoured divisions, reducing them to one tank brigade, one motorised infantry battalion, and artillery formation comprising two field, one AT and one AA regiment.

After the capture of Rome in early June 1944, Alexander had the US 1st, Canadian 5th, British 6th and South African 6th Armoured divisions for use. In Italy, the use of tanks was so impaired by the terrain's rivers and mountains that it was decided to add a second infantry brigade. For example, the British 6th Armoured Division consisted of a tank brigade, a motor brigade and an infantry brigade. As the Allies advanced through the numerous valleys, the heights on either side had to be taken by unwavering infantry units. To overcome logistical hurdles of supply and to afford better protection of accompanying infantry, armoured regiments were equipped with tanks modified as infantry carriers.

The Gothic Line fortification belt in an aerial view along the Highway 65 area that was targeted by US II Corps under Major-General Geoffrey Keyes. The combat waged in the Northern Apennines' undulating peaks and ravines, with limited road access amid mountain-based rivers, was a challenge to an infantryman's campaign. The southern face of this Northern Apennine position was described as 'hostile' as it dropped sharply into the Arno River valley. (*USAMHI*)

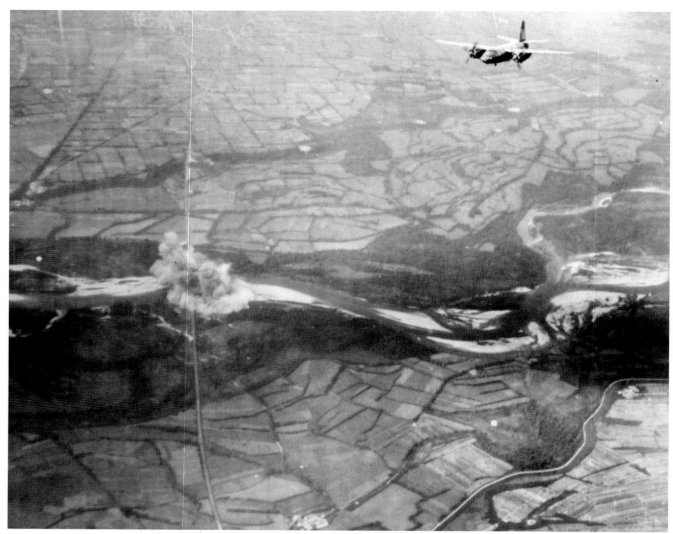

(**Above**) A US 12th Air Force B-26 twin-engined Marauder bombing the Nazi Gothic Line fortifications. Aspects of the Todt Organisation's construction that impeded successful bombardment included the steel and concrete material used along with camouflage that limited detection from above. Additionally, poor weather conditions along the Northern Apennine mountain chain hampered accuracy. (*USAMHI*)

(**Opposite, above**) An aerial view of the Cinquale Canal situated along the Ligurian coastal plain with the foothills of the towering Northern Apennines near Strettoia (*background*). US 92nd ('Buffalo') Division's failed offensive in the Serchio Valley sector of 4–11 February 1945 against the entrenched German 148th Infantry Division occurred in this vicinity. The American attack initially seized some of the high ground. However, 92nd's regiments failed to hold the captured territory in the face of a determined Nazi counter-attack. (*USAMHI*)

(**Opposite, below**) A camouflaged I Canadian Corps' armoured vehicle descending a village's ox-cart track west of Pesaro on the Adriatic coast front in late August 1944. The Canadians were moving into position near the Foglia River to assault the Gothic Line near Osteria Nuova. The armoured vehicle's main gun is wrapped to keep the ubiquitous late-summer road out of the barrel. (*NARA*)

(**Above**) An Eighth Army towed medium field-gun is directed across a stream's temporary Bailey Bridge. The original concrete bridge (*right*) was demolished by retreating Nazis. These 10-foot pre-fabricated steel truss bridge sections, named for the British War Office creator Donald Bailey, were transported to crossings for rapid assembly with simple tools. After the newly erected structure was pushed out across the span, a wood-planking road surface was added, capable of supporting a minimum of 20 tons. The Allies projected a need for 1,000 Bailey bridges to cover the Italian Peninsula to the Po River. However, 3,000 Bailey bridges were erected in less than two years for a total distance of approximately 60 miles. (*NARA*)

(**Opposite**) Despite Kesselring's declaration that Florence was an open city, all of the Arno River's bridges, except for the renowned Ponte Vecchio, were destroyed by the Nazis. Above, Royal Engineers have constructed a Bailey Bridge across the Arno atop the original concrete pylons of the demolished Ponte Santa Trinita, another Renaissance structure, and are laying the wooden planking that will enable vehicular traffic to soon commence in August 1944. The original bridge's construction began in 1566 and was located in between the Ponte Vecchio to the east and the Ponte alla Carraia to the west. (*NARA*)

In Faenza along Highway 9 between Forli and Imola along the Romagna Plain, New Zealand infantry crosses a crude makeshift repair of a demolished steel bridge across the Lamone River in December 1944. Faenza was defended by elements of the Nazi LXXVI Panzer Corps and required a number of Eighth Army formations to capture it. (NARA)

British Eighth Army in the Adriatic coast sector had to cross successive, defended river lines as they moved west towards an entry into the Po Valley and Bologna. Here, a tank officer carefully observes a turretless Churchill Infantry tank variant fording the Montone River, just beyond Forli, on 9 November 1944. The Montone River wound through the Romagna Plain and emptied into the Adriatic Sea to the south of Ravenna. (NARA)

A cloud of dust is generated by a British Eighth Army motorised column along a winding road north of the Montone River near Forli in the Emilia-Romagna region of Italy, while pursuing the Germans in November 1944. Road dust could be seen from a distance, which often brought enemy artillery and mortar fire onto a column. (NARA)

(**Above**) Infantrymen from Company K of the US 91st Division's 362nd Regiment dig their protective foxholes on the reverse slope on a Northern Apennine hilltop on 18 January 1945 near Loiano, in anticipation of a Nazi counter-attack. The Fifth Army's offensive had stalled and another winter's combat of limited engagements ensued amid the snow-covered terrain north of Firenzuola and the Radicosa Pass. (*USAMHI*)

(**Opposite**) British XIII Corps riflemen attached to Fifth Army use a destroyed Italian stone building's rubble as a fortification in Ronta to Florence's north-east during their attack on the Gothic Line that started in mid-September 1944. The British XIII Corps was ceded to Clark by Alexander on account of the American and FEC divisions that left Italy for the southern France invasion. (*NARA*)

A New Zealand infantryman peers around the corner of a building in Faenza from behind a stacked stone fortification. New Zealand, Polish and Indian units all converged on Faenza in December 1944 with their drives across the Lamone River north and south of Highway 9 along the Romagna Plain. (*NARA*)

Soldiers of the US 10th Mountain Division's 86th Mountain Infantry Regiment move along partially snow-covered ground in the Northern Apennines (*background*) to reinforce another of their companies in the Monte Belvedere area of Fifth Army's IV Corps front, on 21 February 1945. The 10th Mountain Division began arriving in Italy on 27 December 1944, and from 19 February to 5 March participated in Operation Encore to seize Monte Belvedere and Monte della Torracia prior to moving onto Vergato on Highway 64, to be in position to move west of Bologna during the upcoming spring offensive. (*USAMHI*)

The US 92nd ('Buffalo') Division's 370th Infantry Regiment's soldiers move along a mountain road past a village on the Fifth Army's IV Corp front on 9 April 1945. The Allied 15th Army Group's spring offensive had commenced and this American formation was conducting a diversionary attack on the Ligurian coast, which began four days previously. Their objective, as they moved through the foothills along the coastal highway, was Massa, which was captured by the US 442nd Japanese-American *Nisei* Regimental Combat Team (RCT) on 11 April. (*USAMHI*)

(**Above**) Infantrymen of the US 91st Division's 363rd Regiment of Clark's Fifth Army manhandle rations up a winding hill path north of the Futa Pass in the Northern Apennines on 27 September 1944, after the Gothic Line was pierced. There were only a few main highways and subsidiary roads through the Northern Apennines for Fifth Army units to reach Bologna and the Po Valley. Months of contentious late autumn and winter combat were to ensue as ammunition, supply and manpower shortages were coupled with harsh weather to stall the Allies for another winter. (*USAMHI*)

(**Opposite, above**) Soldiers from Company B of the US 313th Engineer Battalion clear a mountain path inundated by mud for a British XIII Corps 8th Indian Division's mule-team to move supplies in February 1945 near Monte Grande, 8 miles to the north-east of the village of Livergnano and just west of Route 6528. The main terrain problem confronting Fifth Army's II Corps was the dearth of roads and trails and an endless series of ridges and peaks dominating narrow valleys. Also, the wet late autumn and winter weather turned roadways into quagmires. Only a small amount of ammunition and rations could be mule-carried or manhandled along such paths, which limited the II Corps offensive towards Castel San Pietro situated on Highway 9. (*USAMHI*)

(**Opposite, below**) A mule team starts its uphill climb to supply the US 85th Division's 337th Infantry Regiment in the Northern Apennines near Monte della Formiche on 18 January 1945. The sign along the path reads: 'Mule Track Only. No Jeeps!' These sure-footed pack-animals had once again proven their immense worth to carry supplies to frontline troops in areas scarce of roads. (*USAMHI*)

(**Opposite, above**) A Nazi AT trap along the Gothic Line as it extended across a valley region in the vicinity of Highway 65, near the Futa Pass in the German Fourteenth Army's defensive sector, after the US II Corps attack from 10–18 September 1944. The village of Sant Lucia is situated in the background. (*USAMHI*)

(**Opposite, below**) A week after the Fifth Army's successful offensive, American soldiers observe a long Nazi AT trap near the Gothic Line's Futa Pass's defences on 26 September 1944. The soldiers' presence shows the enormity of the Todt Organisation's AT trap construction, which Kesselring had relied heavily on for the German Fourteenth Army's defence. (*USAMHI*)

(**Above**) A German machine-gun/observation post perched high atop a hill overlooking a valley in the Northern Apennines after its capture on 29 September 1944. Elevated viewpoints aided directing Nazi artillery and mortar fire on Allied troop movements below. The Allies implemented nocturnal attacks and smoke canisters to obscure their troop dispositions. (*NARA*)

Two American soldiers view the corpse of a German soldier near a dug-out in the Northern Apennines on 19 September 1944. The enemy soldier was killed by an artillery company of the US 85th Infantry Division's 338th Regiment upon his Monte Altuzzo position near the important Gothic Line's Il Giogo Pass. (*USAMHI*)

(**Opposite, above**) A German machine-gun position that overlooked a Northern Apennine road in the US II Corps sector. To the gun position's rear was a communicating trench for concealed and protected troop and/or supply reinforcement. (*USAMHI*)

(**Opposite, below**) A German machine-gun position as it was carved into rock, with exterior hessian material camouflaging in the Gothic Line's Monte Altuzzo sector guarding the Il Giogo Pass from the US II Corps 85th Infantry Division's offensive. This elevated enemy position overlooked a valley road below and was captured on 22 September 1944. (*NARA*)

(**Opposite, above**) Infantrymen from the US 85th Division's 339th Regiment look over Nazi weapons and equipment in a captured machine-gun post on a hill on top of a valley region below the Gothic Line's fortifications in the Monte Verucca area on 17 September 1944. The soldier on the left handles an MG 42, while the one on the right examines an enemy radio set. (*USAMHI*)

(**Opposite, below**) The low profile of a turret of a German Panzer Mk V 'Panther' tank emplacement or *Panzerturm* situated along the Futa Pass in the US 91st Division's sector of the Gothic Line's attack in mid-September 1944. This area was defended by elements of the Nazi Fourteenth Army's 4th Parachute Division. These tank turrets were mounted on a reinforced concrete underground bunker. The 'Panther's' 75mm turret gun was a formidable weapon against Allied tanks. (*USAMHI*)

(**Above**) An American bulldozer with crane transports a sunken Nazi pillbox to the rear after it was excavated from a static defence position along the Gothic Line. These portable steel machine-gun posts were utilised along both the Gustav and Gothic Lines with great efficacy against advancing Allied infantry. (*NARA*)

(**Above**) A camouflaged German 150mm heavy field Howitzer (*schwere Feldhaubitze* or sFH 18) gun emplacement that was captured in the US II Corps sector of the Fifth Army's Gothic Line offensive on 14 September 1944. This Howitzer was a mainstay of the *Wehrmacht* and served on all fronts during the war. (*NARA*)

(**Opposite, above**) A German PaK 40 75mm AT gun being examined by American infantrymen along the Gothic Line's fortifications near the Futa Pass in mid-September 1944. This AT emplacement was disabled by US II Corps artillery. The PaK 40 was introduced in February 1942. Its excessive weight necessitated towing. Nonetheless, it was deployed extensively in Italy and was the most commonly deployed Nazi AT cannon during the second half of the war. (*NARA*)

(**Opposite, below**) A German Panzer V 'Panther' disabled by Allied aerial assault along an Italian coastal plain in mid-October 1944. The 'Panther' had its combat debut at the Battle of Kursk on the Eastern Front during the summer of 1943. It combined firepower, armour and manoeuvrability. The 75mm turret gun, which was effective against all Allied armour, was often removed from the chassis of disabled tanks and converted into static *Panzerturms*. (*NARA*)

(**Opposite, above**) Camouflaged artillerymen of the US 10th Mountain Division fire their 75mm pack Howitzer on a snow-covered hilltop. This weapon was developed more than a decade before the American entry into the war for use by mountain divisions. The gun's six components could be quickly disassembled and re-assembled within three minutes as well as manhandled or carried by pack animals, hence the term 'pack Howitzer'. Because of the gun's versatile design, it was also incorporated into Allied paratroop units for airborne assaults with gliders. (*USAMHI*)

(**Opposite, below**) African-American artillerymen of the 598th Field Artillery Battalion attached to the US 92nd ('Buffalo') Infantry Division clean the barrel of their 105mm Howitzer in September 1944 as part of US IV Corps' offensive along the Ligurian coast. The 105mm Howitzer was the division's standard artillery weapon and could be used in an AT role with hollow charge ammunition as proven in North Africa, Sicily, and at Salerno against Panzer counter-attacks. (*USAMHI*)

(**Above**) A Royal Artillery (RA) crew fires an 'air-burst' with their QF, 3.7in heavy AA gun in an uncharacteristic field artillery manner in late August 1944 at enemy Gothic Line positions along the Adriatic coast as part of the start of Eighth Army's Operation Olive in that sector in late August 1944. There was debate over the uncommon use of this weapon in a counter-battery, counter-mortar or AT capacity as the Germans deployed their dual-purpose 88-mm FLAK. The 3.7in guns were used effectively in an AT role, but sparingly, against Panzers in North Africa. During the latter part of the Italian campaign, these 3.7in guns were utilised in a field artillery role. (*NARA*)

(**Opposite, above**) A Canadian artillery crew prepares to fire their camouflaged BL 4.5in medium field cannon (not to be confused with the QF, 4.5in Howitzer or QF, 4.5in anti-aircraft gun) against German fortifications along the Gothic Line in the Adriatic sector during Operation Olive in late August 1944. The earlier Mk 1 was first issued in 1938 and equipped the Royal Artillery (RA) in northern France. Issues of the Mk 2 ordnance started in 1941. Both RA and Canadian gunners utilised this artillery piece effectively in Sicily and elsewhere on the Italian mainland. (*NARA*)

(**Opposite, below**) A Royal Artillery (RA) 155mm cannon crew cover their ears as they fire their weapon against German fortifications along the Gothic Line in late August to early September 1944 during Operation Olive in the Adriatic Sea sector on the Eighth Army front. This 155mm cannon had a maximum range of over 25,000 yards and fired one 200-pound round per minute and was utilised against concrete or steel-reinforced Nazi fortifications. (*NARA*)

(**Above**) A towed British Eighth Army 17-pounder anti-tank (AT) gun moves along a winding road as part of a motorised column raising considerable dust in the Adriatic Sea sector. The column was manoeuvring towards the Foglia River and the Nazi Gothic Line defences in late August 1944 as part of Operation Olive, to pierce the German fortifications there and enter the Romagna Plain. This weapon was one of the best AT guns, incorporating the newly designed armour-piercing, discarding sabot (APDS) along with conventional armour-piercing and high explosive ammunition. The 17-pounder was initially deployed in Tunisia to combat the German Mk VI 'Tiger' tank. (*NARA*)

(**Above**) A British MkI 17-pounder anti-tank (AT) Archer self-propelled gun (SPG) in Cesena in October 1944 during its combat debut. The AT gun was mounted on a Valentine tank chassis and was fixed to fire from a rear-facing position over the engine compartment. Concerns about the rear-facing positions of the gun proved groundless. Attributes of this SPG included its low silhouette and after firing, the armoured vehicle could retreat quickly without having to turn around. This Archer was engaging the enemy across the Savio River near its source at Montes Castelvecchio and Fumaiolo in the Forli-Cesena region before the river coursed 80 miles to the Adriatic Sea in the vicinity of Ravenna. (*NARA*)

(**Opposite, above**) Two American M10 3-inch Gun Motor Carriage (GMC) tank destroyers fire from dug-in positions as conventional artillery. At this stage of the campaign in Italy there were few Nazi armoured counter-attacks, hence the different role for these armoured vehicles. (*NARA*)

(**Opposite, below**) An American M24 Chafee light tank of the 13th Tank Battalion of the US 1st Armoured Division crosses the Po River near Breda on 25 April 1945. As attempts to place a heavier turret gun in M5 light tanks failed, a new design emerged and the M24 was produced by late 1943. The Chaffee light tank possessed a 75mm main turret gun and had a crew of five. It entered into combat in late 1945. (*NARA*)

A pair of Churchill Infantry tanks move along a valley roadway with accompanying infantry atop the armoured vehicle and on the sides of the dusty track. Co-operation between armour and infantry became paramount because of the mountainous terrain and the excellent delaying and containing tactics of the Nazi formations occupying the heights with their armamentarium of AT weapons, necessitating the seizure of these defensive positions by the accompanying ground troops. *(NARA)*

A line of Churchill Infantry tanks abreast of one another overlooking the Foglia River in late August 1944 for the start of Operation Olive to pierce the Gothic Line in the Eighth Army's Adriatic Sea sector. The Churchill possessed tracks that ran around the entire height of the hull in order to enable it to cross wide trenches. During this campaign, the main turret gun was a 6-pounder with later models incorporating a 3-inch gun. The Churchill made a disastrous combat debut along the shingle beaches of Dieppe in support of Canadian assaulting infantry during Operation Jubilee in August 1942. However, it proved useful in the rugged Tunisian terrain in 1943. Its design enabled British tank innovator Percy Hobart to create a number of variants for British sappers called Armoured Vehicle Royal Engineers (AVRE), or Hobart's Funnies, that laid bridges, recovered damaged tanks, filled in ditches, cleared mines, or destroyed fortified bunkers with a heavy mortar in both Italy and north-west Europe. (NARA)

Chapter Three

Commanders and Combatants

General Harold Alexander commanded the Allied 15th Army Group throughout the Sicilian and Italian (until December 1944) campaigns. Prior to that, Alexander was Montgomery's superior during the victories at the Second Battle for El Alamein and across the North African littoral into Tunisia. Then Eisenhower gave him command of the Allied 18th Army Group for the victorious conquest of Tunis and Bizerte in May 1943. Churchill and the entire British military establishment, as well as the American top commanders, viewed Alexander with extreme favour. Churchill recalled, 'Nothing ever disturbed or rattled him, and duty was a full satisfaction in itself, especially if it seemed perilous and hard.' Receiving his field marshal's baton (backdated to the fall of Rome on 4 June 1944), Alexander exuded the quintessential British military *sangfroid*.

The *Luftwaffe's* Field Marshal Albert Kesselring commanded Army Group C in Italy and with Field Marshal Erwin Rommel's departure for France, he was in charge of all German forces throughout the peninsula. Through the Allied slog up the Italian Peninsula, Kesselring had fought one of the best defensive campaigns of any German commander during the war. His outstanding qualities included his strong willpower to motivate his command staff and soldiers at critical times and he demonstrated rapid tactical adaptability at shifting his forces to meet unexpected threats.

Both the US Fifth, under Lieutenant-General Mark Clark, and the British Eighth, under Lieutenant-General Oliver Leese, armies were multinational formations. Thus, neither army was correctly described under its national name. The Fifth Army reflected the coalitions of America, Britain, France and Brazil. Leese, a protégée of Montgomery, took over Eighth Army after his mentor went to London in December 1943 to plan the Normandy ground campaign. His battle honours included El Alamein, Tunis and Sicily with British XXX Corps. Leese was regarded as a capable commander always mindful of the lives of his men, especially with a dwindling British manpower pool at war since 1939. Clark was renowned as an excellent planner, trainer and organiser. Personally brave on the battlefield, he also possessed a knack of attracting publicity. Since Salerno, Clark had a ruffled relationship with his British counterparts as well as some of his own American divisional and corps commanders. His relationship with Alexander was professional and cordial.

The Eighth Army was even more polyglot with expatriate soldiers from Poland, Belgium, Greece and Yugoslavia. The core formations from the United Kingdom and the British Commonwealth included Canadians, New Zealanders, South Africans, Indians, Nepalese Gurkhas and a Jewish Brigade. Italy, as a recent ally after the September capitulation, provided some units.

As of 6 June 1944, the Allies were situated across the waist of Italy from west to east as follows: Fifth Army's US VI Corps, under Major-General Lucian Truscott, comprising the veteran 3rd, 34th and 36th infantries and the 1st Armoured divisions with the tank formation divided into Combat Commands A and B. Further inland was Fifth Army's Major-General Geoffrey Keyes' US II Corps with its 85th and 88th Infantry divisions, commanded by major-generals John Coulter and John Sloan, respectively. These two recently arrived divisions were the first American infantry divisions composed of mostly draftees to enter combat. To the right of US II Corps was the British Eighth Army XIII Corps, under Lieutenant-General Sidney Kirkman. The French Expeditionary Corps' (FEC) four divisions, under General Alphonse Juin, along with the British 78th Division of XIII Corps, were in Fifth and Eighth Army reserve, respectively. British X and V Corps of Eighth Army, under lieutenant-generals Richard McCreery and Charles Allfrey (who was to be replaced by Charles Keightley on 8 August 1944) spanned the Apennines to the Adriatic coast. McCreery was to take over Eighth Army from Leese on 1 October when the latter was sent to command Allied land forces in south-east Asia.

Clark's Fifth Army advance beyond Rome was hampered by frequent regroupings of his divisions as well as transferring the British 1st and 5th divisions back to Eighth Army after their service with US VI Corps at Anzio and the subsequent breakout. Also, as the invasion of southern France was soon to be launched, Clark was going to eventually lose his US VI Corps and FEC divisions (approximately 100,000 troops) in mid-July, along with one-third of his artillery battalions and many Allied air units, for the southern France invasion. Still, Allied firepower and air supremacy remained strong for the campaign's duration.

The divisions earmarked for southern France, though, were battle-hardened veteran formations, with the FEC divisions having recently been lauded for their excellent mountain fighting and *élan* that contributed so greatly to the breaking of the Gustav Line, and would have been of immense utility along the Gothic Line in the Northern Apennines. On 9 June, US IV Corps, under Major-General Willis D. Crittenberger, replaced Truscott's VI Corps along the Tyrrhenian coast. Clark did receive newer American formations, including the US 91st and 92nd ('Buffalo') Infantry divisions. During the first week of August, the Fifth Army was joined by the first elements of the Brazilian Expeditionary Corps of 25,000 men under the command of Major-General João Batista Mascarenhas de Moraes. Although they added to

Clark's numerical strength, they were neither combat-experienced nor prepared for the rigors of campaigning in Italy.

British XIII Corps comprised the British 1st and 8th Indian Infantry and 6th British and 6th South African Armoured divisions. The Polish II Corps, under Lieutenant-General Wladyslaw Anders, had its Kresowa and Carpathian Infantry divisions supported by the Polish 2nd Armoured Brigade. The I Canadian Corps, under Major-General E.L.M. Burns, comprised the 1st Canadian Infantry Division and the 5th Canadian Armoured Division. British X Corps consisted of the 10th Indian Division and the British 9th Armoured Brigade. British V Corps consisted of the British 1st Armoured (new to Italian armoured combat tactics), the British 4th, 46th, 56th Infantry, and the 4th Indian divisions, along with the attached British 7th Armoured and 25th Tank Brigades. Eighth Army also had four free Italian battlegroups, a Jewish Brigade and a Greek Mountain Brigade.

At the Gothic Line on 25 August 1944, the German Tenth Army, under General Heinrich von Vietinghoff, had the veteran LXXVI Panzer Corps, commanded by Lieutenant-General Traugott Herr. The LXXVI Panzer Corps had five infantry divisions, which included the formidable 1st Parachute Division on the Adriatic coast as well as the 278th and 71st Infantry divisions, the 5th Mountain Division with the 26th Panzer Division nearby at Rimini. To the LXXVI Panzer Corps' right were the 51st Mountain Corps' five divisions under General Valentin Feuerstein, comprising the 44th, 305th, 334th and 715th Infantry divisions, along with the 114th Jaeger Division. Further west, opposite the US Fifth Army, were the German Fourteenth Army's six divisions, under Lieutenant-General Joachim Lemelsen, who replaced the sacked Mackensen on 6 June. Lemelsen was a veteran of the German campaigns in Poland, France and the Soviet Union. From the Ligurian coast east, these divisions included the 20th *Luftwaffe* Field Division, the 16th *Waffen* SS Panzer Grenadier Division, and the 65th Infantry Division comprising the German XIV Panzer Corps, under Lieutenant-General Senger und Etterlin. The I Parachute Corps was situated from Pistoia through the Futa, Radicosa and Il Giogo Passes of the Northern Apennines and it comprised the 356th and 392nd Infantry divisions and the 4th Parachute Division. Kesselring held the German 98th and 94th Infantry divisions in reserve at Bologna and Ravenna, respectively.

On 15 December 1944, a major reorganisation of the Allied High Command occurred as Field Marshal Sir John Dill, the chief of the British Military Mission in Washington, died. The Supreme Allied Commander in the Mediterranean, General Henry Maitland Wilson, replaced Dill. Alexander assumed Wilson's role, while Clark took over 15th Army Group. Truscott returned from France to command Fifth Army. General Richard McCreery remained in command of Eighth Army.

The Germans also had a major restructuring of their command hierarchy. On 23 October, Kesselring was in a motor vehicle accident and his recovery interval effectively removed him from command of Army Group C in Italy. Although, Kesselring returned to duty in late January 1945, Hitler ordered him to take over Field Marshal Gerd von Rundstedt's Army Group B to defend the Rhine River. Vietinghoff briefly took command of Army Group C until he was transferred to the Russian front in late January and then returned later in March to permanently replace Kesselring. Lemelsen commanded German Tenth Army in Vietinghoff's absence and he was then replaced in that position by Herr on 17 February. The German Fourteenth Army's leadership also changed hands until Lemelsen returned in late February.

During the autumn of 1944, the northern German-occupied area of Italy had been sporadically plunged into an internal civil war. Following the rescue of Mussolini from Gran Sasso by German glider troops in September 1943, the Italian fascist leader had established a new republic with its base at Salo on Lake Garda. There *Il Duce* lived under German supervision. An Italian partisan movement, led by royalist officers and former Italian prisoners-of-war, rose up against this 'Salo Republic' in the Po Valley becoming major concern for the Nazis by April 1944. The Germans chose to utilise Italian troops still loyal to Mussolini to combat the partisans. Four Italian divisions undergoing training in Germany were to be aligned with three *Wehrmacht* divisions to become the Ligurian Army, based near La Spezia under the former Italian Tenth Army commander from North Africa, Marshal Graziani. This military force, although of potential use against any Allied move on the Alpine passes, was essentially to wage war against the partisan insurrection. Partisan activities behind the German Northern Apennine lines in the Po Valley were so widespread that the Fourteenth Army's XIV Panzer Corps commander, Senger und Etterlin, commented, 'Every time I drove … through a guerilla-infested district, I [was] in the little Volkswagen and displayed no general's insignia of rank.'

(**Above**) Winston Churchill (*centre*) salutes an honour guard, accompanied by the US Fifth Army's commanding general, Clark (*left*), at Cecina in late August 1944, days before the Gothic Line assault. With Alexander a few days later near the Metauro River, Churchill observed first-hand some of the fighting and quipped, '... this was the nearest I got to the enemy and the time I heard the most bullets in the Second World War'. (*NARA*)

(**Opposite, above**) The triumvirate of British military commanders leans on a *Panzerturm* at the Gothic Line in September 1944. From left-to-right: Eighth Army's commander, Leese, Allied 15th Army Group leader, Alexander; and his chief of staff, Lieutenant-General John Harding. These three masterminded Operation Diadem's break-through of the Gustav Line in May 1944 and now implemented Operation Olive, which pierced the Gothic Line in the Eighth Army's Adriatic sector. (*NARA*)

(**Opposite, below**) General Richard McCreery (*right*), the new commander of Eighth Army (Leese departed for south-east Asia on 1 October 1944) with his subordinate commanders on 24 November near Villanova. McCreery was a former cavalry officer and chief of staff for Alexander in the Middle East. At Salerno and north to the Garigliano River, McCreery commanded British X Corps, which comprised initially of the British 46th and 56th Infantry divisions but later augmented to include the British 5th Division for the January 1944 river assault. He was a critic, among many others, of Clark's proposed abandonment of the US VI Corps sector and re-embarkation along the British X Corps front north of the Sele River on 13 September 1943 in the face of strong Nazi counter-attacks at Salerno. Animus between McCreery and Clark continued throughout the Italian campaign. (*NARA*)

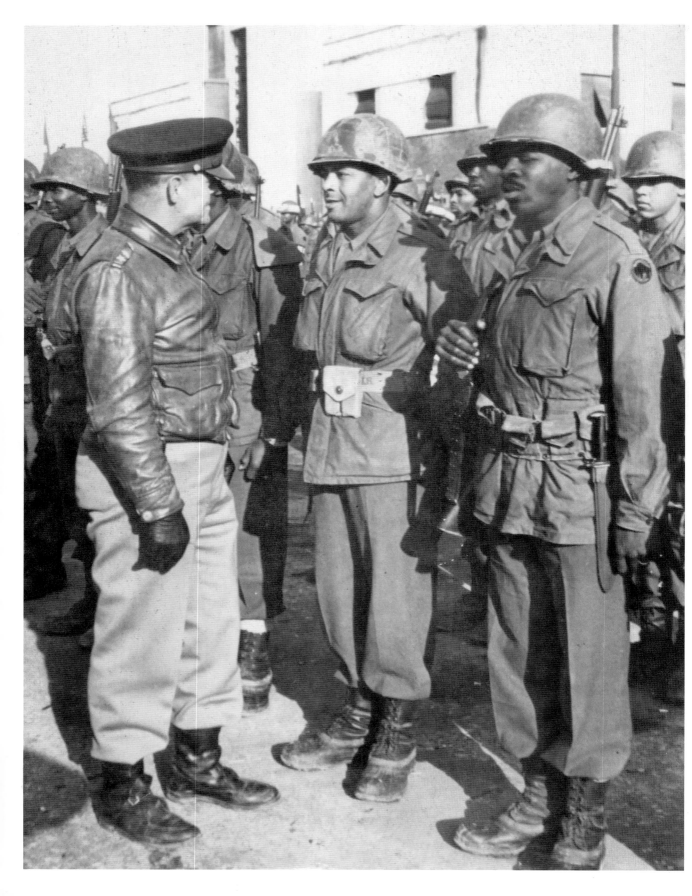

(**Opposite**) The new US Fifth Army commander, Truscott, reviews troops of his African-American 92nd ('Buffalo') Division in January 1945. In 1942, Brigadier-General Truscott was pivotal in the development of the US Ranger battalions in the United Kingdom. During the north-west Africa invasion in November 1942, Truscott commanded a sub-task force and captured the Mehdia-Port Lyautey area to secure the northern flank of Patton's main western task force's assault on Morocco's Atlantic coast. Soon thereafter, Eisenhower appointed Truscott as his deputy chief of staff and representative for operations in Tunisia to amalgamate former Vichy French forces into the inter-Allied order of battle. After success during the bitter Tunisian campaign, Truscott was promoted to lead the 3rd Infantry Division in the invasion of Sicily and spearheaded Patton's Seventh Army advances to Agrigento, Palermo and along the northern coast to Messina. In January 1944, during Operation Shingle, Truscott landed his veteran 3rd Infantry Division along the beaches of Anzio, as part of the US VI Corps amphibious assault. In late February, he took over VI Corps command from Major-General John Lucas, who was relieved. After commanding VI Corps in the southern France invasion in August 1944, Truscott returned to Italy to command Fifth Army, when Clark was promoted to lead the Allied 15th Army Group as Alexander assumed the role as Supreme Commander, MTO. (*NARA*)

(**Above**) Major-General Willis Crittenberger, commanding general of US IV Corps, congratulates members of a Brazilian Expeditionary Force patrol. The Brazilian commander, Major-General João Batista Mascarenhas de Moraes, is also shown (*far right*). Crittenberger, a former cavalryman, had served as chief of staff of the 1st Armoured Division, commanding general of the 2nd Armoured Division, and later commanded the II Armoured Corps. He brought his IV Corps headquarters to Naples in late March 1944 and took over Truscott's VI Corps' frontlines in early June 1944, as the latter corps was to invade southern France in August 1944. (*Author's Collection*)

Major-General Geoffrey Keyes, US II Corps commander, walks across a Treadway Bridge over the Po River in late April 1945. Keyes was a West Point graduate, a veteran cavalryman, and was regarded as an 'intellectual soldier'. Prior to being the deputy commander of Seventh Army, under Patton, during the invasion of Sicily, Keyes was his mentor's deputy in I Armoured Corps in north-west Africa after Bradley assumed command of II Corps in Tunisia. After the 3rd Infantry Division captured Agrigento with Patton's famous 'reconnaissance in force', Keyes commanded a provisional corps in Sicily, which seized Palermo on 22 July 1943 in a matter of days. In January 1944, Keyes led II Corps' 34th and 36th Infantry divisions, the former crossing the Rapido River north of Cassino, and almost succeeded in capturing the monastery in early February, while the latter had two regiments decimated during its Rapido assault south of the town on 20–22 January. For Operation Diadem in May, Keyes commanded the 85th and 88th Infantry divisions along the Tyrrhenian coast. Then, with the additions of 34th and 91st Infantry divisions and the attached 6th South African Armoured Division, Keyes led the assault on the Gothic Line and the Northern Apennines. (NARA)

Field Marshal Harold Alexander (*left*), commanding general of the Allied 15th Army Group, salutes the Polish colours with the II Polish Corps commander, General Wladyslaw Anders, after the victory at Cassino. After a horrendous trek from the Soviet Union through Persia to British lines in the Middle East, the Polish soldiers under his command assaulted Cassino during the final battle there in May 1944. For the Gothic Line assault, Anders' 3rd Carpathian and 5th Kresowa Infantry divisions, supported by 2nd Polish Armoured Brigade, were to advance against tough Nazi parachutist opposition along the Adriatic coast. (*NARA*)

I Canadian Corps commanding general, Lieutenant-General Eedson L. Burns, talking with Major-General Chris Vokes, commanding general 1st Canadian Infantry Division. Burns, an intellectual officer, led the Canadians during the Liri Valley campaign against the Hitler Line following the collapse of the Gustav Line in mid-May 1944. However, he had difficulties interacting with both his British commanders and subordinate Canadian divisional leaders. Burns led his corps next against the Gothic Line in the Adriatic sector as part of Operation Olive. He was replaced by Lieutenant-General Charles Foulkes on 5 November 1944 until the end of the war. (*NARA*)

Major-General John L.T. Hawkesworth (*left*), commanding general of the British 46th Division, aboard USS *Biscayne* with US Navy Rear Admiral Richard L. Conolly (*right*) on 6 September 1943 before the Salerno assault. Hawkesworth was a capable tactician, having led his division at the British X Corps' Garigliano River assault in January 1944. McCreery stated that Hawkesworth 'varied his methods and was always ready to encourage surprise, a silent night approach, and fieldcraft'. Hawkesworth handled his 46th Division well in the British V Corps across the Gothic Line assault and the subsequent combat along the Romagna Plain. (*NARA*)

Colonel William O. Darby (*far left*), as commanding officer of the 179th Infantry Regiment of the US 45th Division, receives a Distinguished Service Order from Eighth Army Commander Leese at San Marco on 7 April 1944. Darby, a West Point graduate, initially started soldiering in the army's last horse artillery unit. During 1942, Darby trained an American infantry unit patterned on the British Commandos, which received the moniker 'Darby's Rangers'. Truscott chose the elite group's name from Rogers Rangers that fought in the pre-revolutionary American colonies. Darby went on to command the 1st Ranger Battalion that assaulted French coastal forts at Arzew as part of the central task force's operations to seize Oran. Truscott said of Darby, 'Never in this war have I known a more gallant, heroic officer.' Darby's Ranger battalions saw extensive combat at Gela with the US 1st Infantry Division on Sicily in July 1943 and as part of Keyes' Provisional Corps too that seized Palermo. At Salerno in September 1943, Darby's Rangers were utilised in an elite capacity to seize and hold the important heights at the Chiunzi Pass after landing at Maiori to the west of Salerno along the northern coast of the Gulf of Salerno in the British X Corps sector. On 30 January 1944, most of Darby's Rangers were killed or captured by the Hermann Göring Division south of Cisterna. The remaining Rangers were absorbed into Brigadier-General Robert Frederick's Canadian-American Special Service Force. Darby became the 45th Division's 179th regimental commander during the Anzio campaign. After a staff job re-assignment, Darby was once again called into action by Major-General George Hays, the 10th Mountain Division commanding general, who wanted Darby as his assistant division commander. When the 10th Mountain Division's Task Force Darby reached the north-eastern end of Lake Garda just days before the final surrender of the Nazis in Italy, Colonel Darby was, as usual, leading from the front, and was killed by a random enemy artillery shell on 30 April 1945, tragically ending a gallant military career. (*USAMHI*)

Captain Charles Candy of the US 92nd Infantry ('Buffalo') Division, under the command of Major-General Edward Almond, seated at the steering wheel of a Jeep on 3 August 1944. Candy led Company F of the 370th Infantry Division on a patrol across the Arno River resulting in the capture of German prisoners the night before near Pontedera. The 370th Regiment was to continue its gallant combat service throughout the remainder of the Italian campaign. Despite some military setbacks, this division was awarded three Legions of Merit and thirteen Silver Stars for gallantry in action. (NARA)

Lieutenant Roland Gagnon with some of his men from the 442nd Japanese-American *Nisei* Regimental Combat Team (RCT) in the Leghorn area on 19 July 1944. General Ryder's 34th Infantry Division relieved the US 36th Division on the Tyrrhenian coast on 26 June. Ryder's veterans of North Africa, Cassino and Anzio had the 442nd RCT attached to it as its centre formation after the Japanese-American soldiers replaced the 517th Parachute Infantry Regiment (PIR), which was scheduled for the southern France invasion. The 442nd RCT was to become one of the mostly highly decorated units of the war. (*NARA*)

An assault squad of infantrymen from Company K of the 87th Mountain Infantry Regiment of the 10th Mountain Division takes cover along a road in the Sassamolare area on 4 March 1945 weeks before Alexander's spring offensive into the Po Valley began. Several American units were combating the Nazis in the Northern Apennines during the winter months at a variety of locales to serve as springboards for the upcoming offensive. The 10th Mountain Division was activated as the 10th Light Infantry (Pack, Alpine) on 15 July 1943, and received specialised training in combat conditions across snow-covered and mountainous terrain, and was redesignated a mountain division on 6 November 1944. It completely arrived in Italy on 18 January 1945. This unit had American skiers, mountain climbers, forest rangers, park/wildlife officers. On 3 March 1945, the division's 86th and 87th Mountain Infantry regiments made a limited offensive to capture the heights west of Highway 64 at Monte Terminale, Monte Della Vedetta, and Monte Acidola. The 85th Mountain Regiment attacked on 5 March and seized Monte Della Spe. On 9 March, the division tactically improved its positions north of Castelnuovo by capturing Montes Valbura and Belvedere. The 10th Mountain emerged from the Northern Apennines into the Po Valley on 20 April. (*USAMHI*)

A soldier from the 363rd Infantry Regiment of the 91st Division rests after man-handling a heavy pack up steep terrain on a ration-carrying detail north of the Futa Pass on 27 September 1944. The 91st, activated in August 1942, arrived in North Africa on 10 May, with its 361st Infantry Regiment disembarking at Anzio on 1 June where it aided the 36th Division's attack on Velletri. This regiment began its advance north of Rome on 12 June, and the 363rd Regiment entered combat on 4 July. This regiment reached the outskirts of Leghorn on 18 July and entered Pisa on 24 July. The remaining two regiments of the division reached the Arno River at Pontedera on 21–22 July. The 91st was heavily engaged in the attack on the Gothic Line at such locales as Monte Monticelli (12–18 September), Monte Calvi (14–18 September), through the Futa Pass, and battling for the Livergnano Escarpment (9–15 October). (USAMHI)

Eighth Army pipers parade through the square in the Republic of San Marino on 27 September 1944. San Marino is situated in the Northern Apennines as the mountains begin to descend onto the ridges and rivers along the Romagna Plain to the south-west of Rimini on the Adriatic Coast. San Marino is one of the world's oldest republics and this tiny Italian city-state's neutral status was respected by Kesselring in his instructions to the German Tenth Army commander, Vietinghoff. (NARA)

(**Above**) Eighth Army sappers using metal detectors to uncover planted landmines on a road leading into the Republic of San Marino. On 28 July 1943, three days after the fall of Benito Mussolini, fascist rule in San Marino collapsed as the local government proclaimed its neutrality in the war. Although the fascists regained power in San Marino in April 1944, they respected the republic's neutrality. The local government on 26 June declared that there were no weapons of war within the tiny republic. Despite that, San Marino was briefly occupied by German forces in September 1944, who were defeated by Eighth Army forces after the Gothic Line crossing. (*USAMHI*)

(**Opposite, above**) An Anglo-American ground-to-air tactical control team reviews map co-ordinates in the Northern Apennine south of Bologna on 1 December 1944 during the autumn-to-spring stalemate in the mountains north of the Gothic Line. The inclement weather and cloud cover interfered with the target co-ordination for Allied fighter-bombers, which contributed to limited Allied advances in the mountains. (*USAMHI*)

(**Opposite, below**) A British Eighth Army Vickers machine-gun crew in action along the Adriatic sector in late August 1944. The machine-gunners were involved in providing indirect fire support for the infantry crossing the Adriatic coastal plain combating the Nazi 1st Parachute and 278th Infantry divisions just south of the Gothic Line near the port of Pesaro. (*NARA*)

(**Above**) A British Eighth Army infantry section moves through the ruins of an Italian village in the Adriatic sector during the battle for the Gothic Line in late August 1944. Amid the rubble is a destroyed Universal Carrier. *(NARA)*

(**Opposite, above**) A column of the 2nd Battalion Royal Inniskilling Fusiliers march past some of their entrenched comrades in the Po Valley in mid-April 1944. The Royal Inniskilling Fusiliers were an Irish line infantry regiment of Eighth Army. After the Gothic Line battles and the ensuing winter stalemate along the Senio River in the Romagna Plain, this regiment absorbed many soldiers of the 6th Battalion and was transferred to the 38th (Irish) Infantry Brigade of the 78th Infantry Division that played a prominent role in clearing the town of Argenta just prior to the breakout into the Po Valley. *(Author's Collection)*

(**Opposite, below**) Canadian stretcher-bearers wear Red Cross bands on their left arms while carrying an injured infantryman under fire near the Gothic Line in early September 1944. The I Canadian Corps was advancing in the Adriatic sector between the II Polish Corps on the coast and the British V Corps along the foothills of the Northern Apennines. *(NARA)*

(**Above**) A Canadian 5th Armoured Division M7 'Priest' 105mm Gun Motor Carriage (GMC), as part of the I Canadian Corps, advances towards the Gothic Line in early September 1944. The extensive road dust necessitated the GMC crewmen to cover the 105mm Howitzer barrel as well as the 0.50-inch calibre machine-gun in the open gun turret on the left side of the armoured vehicle. (*NARA*)

(**Opposite, above**) After piercing the Gothic Line's defences, a Canadian Reconnaissance Unit's lightly armoured vehicles carry the wounded amid sniper fire down a lane in an Italian village along the Marecchia River, which flowed to the seaside port of Rimini to the north-east in mid-September 1944. The Canadians went on to capture Rimini on 21 September. The next day, the 2nd New Zealand Division, which had been in Eighth Army reserve, passed through the 1st Canadian Infantry Division and crossed the Marecchia as Alexander and Leese's *corps de chasse* to pursue the retreating Germans to the north-west. The New Zealanders battered the German 162nd Turkoman Division, which was recruited from former Soviet sources on the Russian front. However, they then encountered the main body of the German 1st Parachute Division, which halted the New Zealand advance. (*NARA*)

An Eighth Army Canadian 25-pounder field-gun crew from Newfoundland prepares its weapon for action along the Adriatic sector in September 1944, as part of the advance on Rimini after breaking through the Gothic line on the left flank of the Poles advancing along the coast from Ancona to Pesaro. (*NARA*)

(**Opposite, above**) Infantrymen of the 3rd Algerian Infantry Division of General Juin's French Expeditionary Corps (FEC) man a light machine-gun position as part of the Clark's Fifth Army front. Upon moving north from Rome in early June, the FEC advanced with the US II Corps' 85th and 88th divisions. However, Juin's FEC, which had fought so well in the mountains north of Cassino in late January–early February 1944 and broke through the Gustav Line in the south to the right of II Corps in mid-May, were to leave Italy for the August 1944 invasion of southern France. (*NARA*)

(**Above**) A New Zealand infantry section passes through the ruins of Faenza on 23 December 1944, after Eighth Army formations captured the town situated between the Lamone and Senio rivers on Highway 9 in the Romagna Plain. The initial attack on Faenza was made by the British V Corps' 4th and 46th divisions and was launched on 21 November, with the Germans withdrawing behind the Lamone and Marzeno rivers on 23–24 November. (*NARA*)

(**Opposite, below**) A New Zealand 23rd Battalion Bren gun team inside a fortified position in Faenza approximately 400 yards from the enemy. The winter weather was setting in as evidenced by the two New Zealand soldiers wearing woollen watch caps. The German 26th Panzer Division, reduced to 1,000 men, was still able to hold on to parts of the city despite the convergence of a number of different Eighth Army divisions by mid-December. (*NARA*)

(**Opposite, above**) After Faenza was captured by different Eighth Army units, four New Zealand infantrymen find some comic relief amid the ruins of the city as they regard a sign posting a 'gallows humour' warning on 23 December 1944. (*NARA*)

(**Opposite, below**) A New Zealand infantry patrol garbed in winter-white camouflage uniforms as it moves across a snow-covered field in mid-January 1945. In late October, the MTO's supreme commander, Wilson, warned the combined chiefs of staff that the 15th Army Group offensive was soon to halt resulting from an infantry manpower shortage with the onset of winter conditions. By 6 January, winter weather had set in with a vengeance, characterised by blizzards and heavy snowfall in both the mountains and across the Romagna Plain. Nonetheless, sporadic limited offensives and active patrolling became the norm until the spring offensive of April 1945 to outflank the enemy positions in the Adriatic sector at the Argenta Gap and break into the Po Valley. (*NARA*)

(**Above**) Infantrymen of the 6th South African Armoured Division come out of their foxholes after six winter days and nights in the Northern Apennines as part of US IV Corps. Earlier in the campaign to the north of Rome, the South Africans, as part of British XIII Corps, liberated Orvieto in late June 1944 and participated in the Battle for Florence south of the city from 30 July to 1 August. (*USAMHI*)

(**Above**) A 6th South African Armoured Division's M4 medium tank with infantry aboard as it moves out of the Northern Apennines towards Bologna on 20 April 1945. The 6th South African Armoured and US 1st Armoured divisions were part of the US IV Corps. (*USAMHI*)

(**Opposite, above**) A supply train of the Royal Indian Service Corps' 2nd Mule Company carries supplies for the British 46th Infantry Division on 2 October 1944 during the Battle of the Rivers combat between Rimini and Cesena along Highway 9. The Gothic Line assault had been victorious, but the crossing of the successive parallel rivers towards Bologna along Highway 9 was gruelling and drained the Eighth Army of ammunition and manpower. (*USAMHI*)

(**Opposite, below**) Infantrymen from a Punjabi battalion of British XIII Corps' 8th Indian Division attached to Clark's Fifth Army ascend steep stones near a small waterfall in the Northern Apennines during the late autumn of 1944. Numerous heights had to be ascended by XIII Corps as they manoeuvred as the right flank of Fifth Army towards Imola on Highway 9 and the Romagna Plain. (*USAMHI*)

(**Opposite, above**) Indian artillerymen train with a captured German PaK 40 75mm AT gun in November 1944. It was seized as the 8th Indian Division advanced as part of British XIII Corps on the right flank through the Northern Apennines until cold weather, heavy snow and severe shortages produced a stalled offensive to Bologna and the Po Valley for another Italian winter. (*NARA*)

(**Opposite, below**) A grinning Nepalese infantryman from a 4th Indian Division Gurkha unit in British V Corps brandishes his combat knife, or *kukri*, in the Coriano Ridge area near Rimini in September 1944. The Gurkhas also fought fiercely for Gemmano to pierce the Gothic Line. (*NARA*)

(**Above**) A corporal in a 4th Indian Division Gurkha unit of British V Corps readies his Thompson 0.45-inch calibre submachine-gun during the house-to-house combat for Sant Arcangelo di Romagna. This town, situated on Highway 9 on the Romagna Plain between Rimini on the Adriatic coast and Cesena, was contested by the German LXXVI Panzer Corps' 26th Panzer Division during the early phase of the Battle of the Rivers as Eighth Army began their slow advance past successive enemy defended river lines towards Bologna. (*NARA*)

(**Above**) A German propaganda photograph shows Polish soldiers as they start their march into captivity after the German conquest and Soviet entry into the eastern half of Poland. Those Polish soldiers who did not perish at the hands of the Soviets were released to begin another intercontinental trek to join British forces in the Middle East, where they were fed, kitted and armed to become the fighting units of the II Polish Corps dispatched to Italy in late 1944. (*Author's Collection*)

(**Opposite, above**) II Polish Corps sappers bridge a river in the Adriatic sector in autumn 1944. The Poles had captured Ancona on the coast and, after fighting through the Gothic Line's defences as part of Eighth Army's effort, General Anders' divisions moved west along the Romagna Plain after the capture of Rimini on 21 September. The Polish Corps had to then contend with numerous river crossings during their north-westward movement towards Faenza. (*Author's Collection*)

(**Opposite, below**) Italian Colonel Jianinni with his 4th Battalion Pack Mule Company ready for departure to the front in the Comoggiano area in the Ligurian coast sector in February 1945. Some of the Italian units that joined the Allies fought admirably against both the Nazis and their fellow fascist countrymen. However, other formations were ill-equipped and ill-suited for combat. (*USAMHI*)

A Brazilian Expeditionary Force 81mm mortar crew of the Heavy Weapons Company, 2nd Battalion, 1st Regiment fighting as part of US IV Corps loads a round for a fire mission in support of its infantry in the Sassomolare area on 16 April 1945. During November 1944, General João Batista Mascarenhas de Morales' Brazilian Expeditionary Force was brought up to division-strength with the arrival of the 1st and 11th Infantry regiments. These were the first units from any South American country ever to fight on European soil. (*USAMHI*)

An AT unit of the Jewish Brigade fighting in Eighth Army at inspection in the Po Valley in April 1945. From left-to-right were a Briton, a Hungarian, a Russian, a Czech, an Austrian, a Palestinian Jew, an Egyptian and a Pole. The brigade was comprised of three Palestine regiments and included armoured vehicles and artillery units. (*Author's Collection*)

Captain Abraham Akavia, an officer in the Eighth Army's Jewish Brigade, at his desk at a headquarters locale. Akavia was a member of Orde Wingate's Special Night Squads during the Arab Revolt in Palestine in 1938. He accompanied Wingate to Ethiopia as an *aide de camp* to combat the Duke of Acosta's Italian forces there with a locally raised pro-Selassie guerilla unit in the Gojjam Province, Gideon Force, in early 1941. As the Ethiopian patriots made progress against the Italians in the Gojjam, Wingate prophetically mentioned to Akavia that the success of Gideon Force was directly relevant to the ultimate formation of a Jewish fighting force. Wingate, the future leader of the *Chindits* in Burma, had hoped to form such a combat group as he was fiercely pro-Zionist, an unusual political position for a British Army officer. (*NARA*)

Eighth Army infantrymen of the 3rd Greek Mountain Brigade fighting in Rimini, which they and Canadian soldiers captured on 21 September 1944. At the start of Operation Olive, on 25 August, the 3rd Greek Mountain Brigade was newly arrived from the Middle East and held in Eighth Army reserve. On 6 September, Leese committed it from reserve status to the I Canadian Corps for a major assault across the Marano River. Two weeks later, after a battle around an airfield near Rimini, the Greeks lost 314 men. On the night of 20 September, the Germans destroyed their ammunition dumps in Rimini and the following morning the Greek and Canadian flags were hoisted above the Rimini town hall. In early October, as civil war broke out in Greece after the Nazi evacuation, Alexander and Wilson dispatched the remaining soldiers of the 3rd Mountain Brigade along with the 4th Indian Division to Athens to bolster the Royal Army fighting the ELAS communist guerrilla faction. (*Author's Collection*)

German General Heinrich von Vietinghoff, a First World War veteran and aggressive Russian front Panzer commander, served as commanding general of the Nazi's Tenth Army throughout the Italian campaign after the Allied invasion of Sicily. His armoured counter-attacks at Salerno almost forced Clark to evacuate his US VI Corps beachhead in September 1943, whereas his static defence along the Volturno River enabled completion of the Gustav Line, behind which his Tenth Army tenaciously resisted the Allied 15th Army Group from the Tyrrhenian coast to Cassino, delaying the advance onto Rome for five months. North of Rome, his Tenth Army staunchly defended its sector of the Gothic Line in the Northern Apennines and along the Romagna Plain prior to the Allied breakout into the Po Valley at the end of April 1945. (*Author's Collection*)

(**Left**) General Joachim Lemelsen, the German Fourteenth Army commander, had extensive experience. He participated in the invasions of Poland and France in 1939 and 1940, respectively, before commanding the XLVII Motorised Corps during Operation Barbarossa in 1941 and at the Battle of Kursk in 1943. After a First Army command on France's Atlantic Coast, he replaced Mackensen as Fourteenth Army commander in Italy in early June 1944. Lemelsen contended with manpower shortages defending the Gothic Line and the Northern Apennines and his forces were not of equal quality to Vietinghoff's Tenth Army, especially after they had been mauled during the retreat from Anzio to the Arno River. (*Author's Collection*)

(**Centre**) General Traugott Herr, commanding general of the German LXXVI Panzer Corps. At Salerno, after successfully disengaging his 29th Panzer Grenadier and 26th Panzer divisions from Montgomery's Eighth Army's slow advance, he delivered sharp Panzer counter-attacks against the Allied beachhead on 13 September 1943 that compelled Clark to consider evacuation of the US VI Corps sector south of the Sele River. Along the Gothic Line and Romagna Plain in the Adriatic sector, he led to divisions in a spirited defence that produced another winter's stalemate in the Italian campaign. (*Author's Collection*)

(**Right**) Lieutenant-General Fridolin von Senger und Etterlin took over the command of German XIV Corps from Hube in late autumn of 1943 in time for the intense conflicts culminating in the First Battle of Cassino. Intriguingly, Senger und Etterlin had strong roots in Catholicism as well as being a lay Benedictine, which was pertinent since he was to command the defences involved in the Monte Cassino battles. Senger und Etterlin was an Oxford-educated officer who fought for his country over his odds with Hitler's brutal regime. A First World War veteran artilleryman and a post-war Weimar cavalryman, Senger und Etterlin led a brigade during the *blitzkrieg* in France in May 1940 and the 17th Panzer Division during the winter campaign of 1942 on the Russian front. On Sicily, he liaised with the Italian forces poorly defending their soil. After the withdrawal from Cassino and the fall of Rome, Senger und Etterlin continued to command the XIV Panzer Corps as part of the German Fourteenth Army, along its sector of the Gothic Line and Northern Apennines between the Ligurian Army to the north-east and the I Parachute Corps defending the important Futa and Il Giogo Passes opposite the US II Corps. He represented Vietinghoff at the formal surrender ceremony to Generals Clark, McCreery and Truscott at Allied headquarters at Caserta on 5 May 1945. (*NARA*)

German General Richard Heidrich, commander of the *Luftwaffe*'s 1st Parachute Division. Veterans of Cassino, this elite formation fought tenaciously as part of Herr's LXXVI Panzer Corps between Pesaro and Rimini and then along the Romagna Plain. Heidrich served in France, Crete and at Leningrad before assuming command of the 1st Parachute Division, which he led in Sicily and southern Italy before being deployed for the several months-long Cassino defence. He was promoted to command the I Parachute Corps in early 1945. (*Author's Collection*)

Two future German field marshals with Adolf Hitler during the Polish *blitzkrieg*. Saluting the Nazi dictator was the *Luftwaffe's* General Albert Kesselring, who had proven his tactical mettle by incorporating his *Stuka* squadrons as 'flying artillery' for the infantry's rapid advances. Between Hitler and Kesselring was Major-General Erwin Rommel, who commanded Hitler's bodyguard battalion and his field headquarters during the invasion of Poland, which started on 1 September 1939. The two officers were to disagree on tactics, strategy and supply, when Rommel landed in Tripoli to command the new *Deutsches Afrika Korps* (DAK) in February 1941. In Italy, in 1943, the two field marshals again had opposing views of where to fight the invading Allied armies after the loss of Sicily in mid-August. With Rommel's posting to France, Kesselring's strategy to fight the Allies south of Rome was implemented with Hitler's approval. (*Author's Collection*)

A German propaganda photograph documents the *esprit* of the young *Wehrmacht* troops marching off to the invasion of Poland in 1939. For more than three years, the German Army divisions were not to suffer any catastrophic setbacks until Stalingrad and El Alamein. *(Author's Collection)*

German parachutists manning a mortar on the Gothic Line in late summer 1944. Although Heidrich's 1st Parachute Division was exemplary in all of its battles, other units, such as the 4th Parachute Division in the Fourteenth Army, which was tasked with the defence of the vital approaches to the Il Giogo Pass north of Florence, were not as formidable, as the bulk of the division were no longer the veterans of Anzio but rather composed of very young soldiers with only three months' training. *(Author's Collection)*

German prisoners captured by the US 10th Mountain Division's 87th Mountain Infantry Regiment are escorted into captivity. Although prisoners, the Germans still exhibit confidence, which contributed greatly to the delay they imposed on the Allied Fifth and Eighth armies as they struggled to get through the Northern Apennines and Romagna Plain to gain access to the Po Valley and northern Italy. *(USAMHI)*

Chapter Four

From Rome to the Arno

Following the evacuation of Rome on 4 June 1944, the Nazi Fourteenth Army retreated amid roads clogged with vehicles and *Wehrmacht* infantry. Two days after Rome fell, Alexander received orders from General Wilson to quickly push the Nazis 170 miles to the north to a line running from Pisa to Rimini and prevent a link-up of the German Fourteenth and Tenth armies and a subsequent concentrated defence. The US Fifth Army's destination was the triangle of Pisa-Lucca-Pistoia along the Arno River. The British Eighth Army, advancing along a front of almost 200 miles from the Adriatic to the interior of the Italian Peninsula, aimed for the triangle of Florence-Arezzo-Bibbiena.

Neither Allied army rapidly advanced. Clark's deployment of Fifth Army's three mechanised and eight infantry divisions slowly pursued the defeated Fourteenth Army. Kesselring noted a fact that if Clark had quickly advanced along a broad front rather than concentrate his Fifth Army attack on the junction of both the German armies along the Tiber River, the Nazi Fourteenth Army's position to the north of Rome would have disintegrated. The German 29th and 90th Panzer Grenadier along with the 26th Panzer divisions had occupied the Tiber River crossings between Rome and Orvieto, retarding the US Fifth Army's advance. The northward orderly retreat of the German Fourteenth Army, now under Lemelsen, to either side of Lake Bracciano between Civitavecchia and Civita Castellana, gained time for the Gothic Line's completion and reinforcement of this Nazi army that was mauled at Anzio and along the Caesar Line.

The US IV Corps replaced the VI Corps on 9 June along the Tyrrhenian Sea Coast. The French Expeditionary Corps (FEC) were to remain for several more days to attack Grosseto along the western end of the German temporary defensive belt, the Albert Line, which extended eastwards through Umbria to just north of Perugia. The FEC also captured the island of Elba on 19 June. Juin's troops managed to move north of Lake Bolsena reaching Radicofani on the Albert Line by 18 June before the French 1st Motorised Division left for Naples for redeployment. Although it was only a line of temporary defences, the Albert Line represented a locus where the German Fourteenth and Tenth armies had formed a united Army Group C, instead of possibly being attacked and defeated.

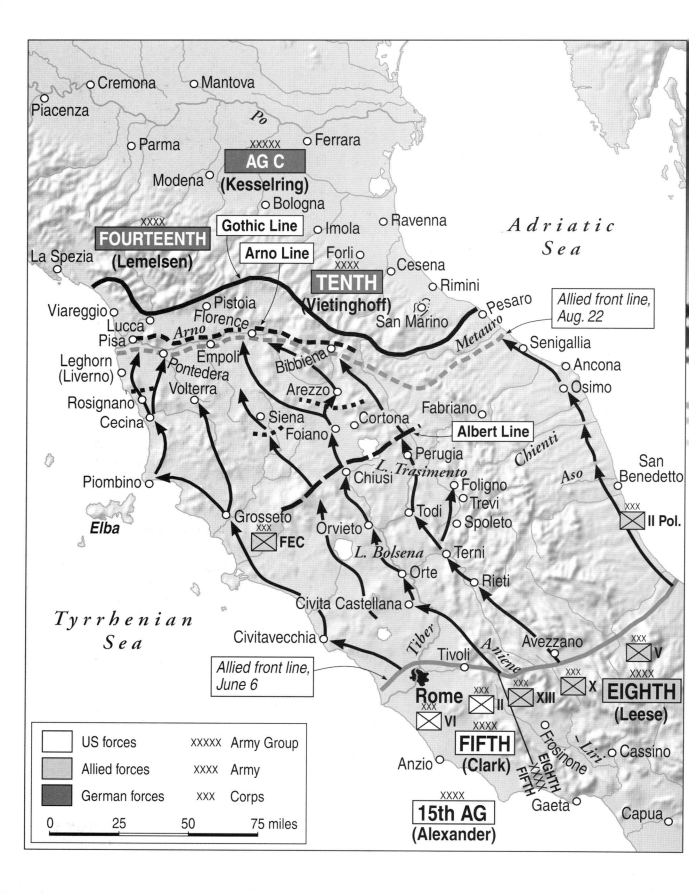

Cremona ○   ○ Mantova

Piacenza ○

○ Parma   *Po*   ○ Ferrara

         Modena ○
                         xxxxx
                         AG C
                         (Kesselring)

                              ○ Bologna

                    Gothic Line   ○ Imola   ○ Ravenna

    xxxx   **Arno Line**   Forlì ○
FOURTEENTH   xxxx   ○ Cesena
(Lemelsen)   **TENTH**   ○ Rimini

La Spezia ○   **(Vietinghoff)**
                                                      ○ San Marino   ○ Pesaro

Viareggio ○   Pistoia ○   *Allied front line,*
          Lucca ○   Florence ○   *Metauro*   *Aug. 22*
Pisa ○   *Arno*   ○ Senigallia
                    Empoli ○   ○ Ancona
Leghorn   Pontedera ○   Bibbiena ○
(Liverno) ○   ○ Osimo
          Volterra ○   Arezzo ○
Rosignano ○   Fabriano ○
Cecina ○   Siena ○   Cortona ○   **Albert Line**
                  Foiano ○   *Chienti*   San
                                        Perugia ○   Benedetto ○
Piombino ○   Chiusi ○ *L. Trasimeno*
                  Grosseto ○   Foligno ○   *Aso*   xxx
                        xxx   Orvieto ○ Todi ○ Trevi ○   **II Pol.**
Elba   **FEC**   Spoleto ○

              L. Bolsena   Terni ○
Tyrrhenian   Orte ○   Rieti ○
    Sea   xxx
                  Civita Castellana ○   Avezzano ○   **V**
          Civitavecchia ○   *Tiber*   xxx   xxxx
    Allied front line,   Tivoli ○ *Aniene*   xxx **XIII** **X** **EIGHTH**
        June 6   xxx   **Rome** **II**   **(Leese)**
                                      Anzio ○   xxx
                                              VI   xxxx   *Lin.*
                                                    FIFTH   Frosinone ○ ○ Cassino
┌──────────────────────────────┐   **(Clark)**
│ ▢ US forces   xxxxx Army Group│   Anzio ○   ○ Gaeta   ○ Capua
│ ▨ Allied forces xxxx Army   │
│ ▨ German forces xxx Corps   │   xxxx
│   │   **15th AG**
│ 0   25   50   75 miles   │   **(Alexander)**
└──────────────────────────────┘

Adriatic
Sea

Tyrrhenian
Sea

On 6 June 1944, the South African 6th Armoured Division, crossing the Aniene River east of Tivoli, captured Civita Castellana. However, their breakthrough was quickly contained by rapidly deployed German reinforcements comprising former Soviet prisoners-of-war in the 162nd Turkomen and the 356th Infantry divisions. The US 34th Division captured Civitavecchia along the Tyrrhenian coast north of Rome on 7 June 1944. The Germans brought an armoured division and the 90th Panzer Grenadier Division to the Lake Bolsena area south-west of Orvieto. Despite the reinforcements, the Nazis had to abandon the Tiber River bridge crossing before Orvieto on 14 June to the South Africans and some FEC motorised elements.

Alexander's 15th Army Group directive from 7 June called for Leese's Eighth Army to attack north-west through the Umbria region and move on Florence on the Arno River via an axis of Perugia-Arezzo-Bibbiena along the foothills of the Northern Apennines. However, a combination of poor terrain, rain and local Nazi resistance delayed the advance of Leese's divisions. Nonetheless, by 21 June, the Nazis had retreated more than 100 miles to the north of Rome. Alexander made the seemingly fatuous prediction that his 15th Army Group would be beyond Bologna and into the Po Valley by the end of the summer months, poised to attack Austria and the Balkans, which fed into Churchill's but not the Americans' strategic scenario.

The US Fifth Army's IV Corps moved up the Tyrrhenian coast and seized several Italian locales. Cecina was captured by the 34th Division on 2 July. The 442nd RCT of Japanese-American *Nisei* seized Leghorn on 19 July and Pisa fell to US IV Corps forces on 23 July. At this point, the US 91st Division, which had entered action for the first time in July, had reached Pontedera on the Arno River on 23 July, while further east the US 88th Division had also reached the river. Fifth Army units were now poised to converge on Florence from the west along an axis of Pisa-Lucca-Pistoia.

Soon after Rome's capture, British XIII Corps achieved some rapid progress on Eighth Army's left flank across the Tiber toward Tivoli. In mid-June, XIII Corps'

Strategic situation. The northern advance of Alexander's Allied 15th Army Group's (AG) Fifth (under Clark) and Eighth (under Leese) armies beyond Rome to the Arno River from their 6 June frontline positions until 5 August 1944 is indicated by bold arrows. US VI (to be replaced by IV Corps on 9 June) and II Corps, along with the French Expeditionary Corps (FEC), comprised the Fifth Army's movement along the Tyrrhenian coast and inland to it. Eighth Army's British XIII, X and V Corps advanced along both sides of the Apennine Mountain spine of the Italian Peninsula, while the II Polish Corps attacked along the Adriatic coast. More temporary Nazi defensive positions (see Chapter Two for details) were situated on both sides of Lake Trasimento (Albert Line) as well as to the south of Siena, Arezzo and Leghorn. The Arno Line, north of the Arno River, ran from Pisa on the west coast to east of Bibbiena. To the north of Florence, along the southern face of the Northern Apennines, was the Gothic Line, a formidable defensive belt, behind which Kesselring's AG C's two German armies, the Fourteenth (under Lemelsen) and Tenth (under Vietinghoff), were situated. The Allied front line, spanning the peninsula, was in position by 22 August for the upcoming Operation Olive. The combat along the Gothic Line ensued from 25 August to 18 September. (*Philip Schwartzberg, Meridian Mapping*)

8th Indian Infantry Division captured Spoleto and Trevi and then pushed on north-ward past Foligno to the south of Perugia. Now Kirkman's troops began to face considerable enemy resistance by the Nazi LXXVI Panzer Corps at the Albert Line near Lake Trasimeno just to the south of Foiano. On 20 June, XIII Corps opened its attack on this makeshift, temporary defensive belt, just south-west of the lake near Chiusi, and required its British 4th and 78th Infantry divisions, the South African 6th Armoured Division and the Canadian 1st Armoured Brigade to break through by 28 June. Foiano was captured on 2 July.

British XIII Corps' next intended destination was Arezzo, a railway hub to the upper Arno area. As Arezzo was a vital supply and reinforcement hub for the Eighth Army, the 8th and 10th Indian Infantry and 2nd New Zealand divisions were added to the assault on 15 July. Despite being defended by elements of the German 1st Parachute, the 334th and 715th Infantry, and 15th Panzer Grenadier divisions, Arezzo was captured on 18 July. The Fifth and Eighth armies had advanced up the Tyrrhenian coast and breached the Albert Line with their movements now poised for the Arno River and Florence.

In contrast to British XIII Corps, the British X Corps was slow in its movement north. It was not until 10 June that, in the centre of the Eighth Army front, it reached Avezzano. Then British X Corps continued on to Rieti and Terni, paralleling the course of the Tiber, on the heels of the doggedly resisting German LXXVI Panzer Corps, and captured Terni and Perugia on 13 and 19 June, respectively.

On the Adriatic sector front, the German withdrawal commenced on 7 June 1944 with British V Corps in pursuit. However, the Abruzzi Apennines were a delaying factor. Ten days later, Polish II Corps relieved the British V Corps. By 20 June, the Poles had crossed the Aso River, but they met strong enemy resistance at the Chienti River. It took the Poles almost three weeks to reach Osimo and, after fierce combat, the Adriatic port of Ancona was captured on 18 July. They then advanced north-west to Senigallia and reached the Metauro River, just south of the Gothic Line, on 22 August, despite resistance by the German 71st and 1st Parachute divisions.

By 22 July, the Allies converging offensives towards Florence commenced. During the night of 2–3 August, the bulk of German forces crossed the lower Arno and occupied newer positions on the river's northern bank. On 4 August, the Indian and New Zealand infantry divisions reached the southern bank of the Arno between Florence and Empoli, while elements of the South African 6th Armoured Division penetrated the Florentine outskirts. Although Kesselring had previously declared Florence an open city, German troops had blown up all the Arno bridges before the Allied arrival on 4 August, except for the historic Ponte Vecchio, to which the roads approaching this monumental structure were rendered impassable by mines and destroyed buildings. Although the Nazis had eight divisions, these formations had limited armour and artillery support and the infantry were reduced in strength.

With Florence captured, Alexander wanted to continue his Eighth Army's left flank offensive to penetrate the Gothic Line and advance on Bologna. However, Clark and Leese halted their formations after Florence's capture to re-fit and rest. From Rome to the Arno River, the Fifth Army sustained approximately 18,000 casualties while the Eighth Army had 16,000. This mid-summer respite enabled Kesselring to re-double his efforts to complete the Gothic Line defences north of the Arno.

The German Tenth and Fourteenth armies, despite numerous losses in both man-power and ordnance, retreated from Rome to the Gothic Line without a catastrophic defeat, remaining intact behind their formidable defensive belt across the desolate Northern Apennines. From mid-June to mid-August, the Germans lost more than 63,000 men killed, wounded, or missing. The Fifth Army captured 16,000 Germans, while the Eighth Army added an additional 7,000. The Italian terrain limited Allied armour to quickly pursue German Army Group C and destroy it. The Allied attack on the Gothic Line was to begin as a surprise assault in the Adriatic sector on the night of 25–26 August 1944.

US infantrymen from the IV Corps' 36th Division's 143rd Regiment move through countryside north of Rome in the Grosseto area, near the Tyrrhenian Sea on a line to the west of Orvieto, on 20 June 1944. The 36th Division was a veteran formation of the Salerno invasion and the ill-fated Rapido River assault at Cassino. This former Texas National Guard unit enabled the capture of Velletri after their nocturnal assault into the Alban Hills after the Anzio breakout less than a month before. The Allied advance north of Rome was not at a brisk pace allowing some Nazi formations to strongly occupy the Tiber River crossing between the Eternal City and Orvieto. (*USAMHI*)

British XIII Corps' 6th South African Armoured Division troops and vehicles enter Orvieto, just to the north of the Tiber, through one of the town's arches, on 14 June 1944. Moving from the east of Rome and crossing the Aniene River, a tributary of the Tiber at Rome, XIII Corps advanced on an axis of Tivoli-Civita Castellana-Orvieto, on the heels of the German 26th Panzer and 90th Panzer Grenadier divisions. The German formations crossed the Tiber River at Orte by 8 June bound for Orvieto the next day. These Nazi units resisted the Allied entry into Orvieto. However, by 14 June, the enemy retreated from the town. (*NARA*)

(**Opposite, above**) An M4 medium tank of the US 1st Armoured Division moves cautiously along a narrow street in Paganico, located in Grosseto Province, on 21 June 1944. This town was along the line of the German Fourteenth Army retreat north of Rome. Three of the Fourteenth Army's divisions, the 65th, 362nd and 715th Infantry formations, were practically destroyed with Nazi columns frequently congesting the narrow roads through the passed-through villages as well. (*USAMHI*)

(**Opposite, below**) A section of British Eighth Army's X Corps infantrymen advancing at a rapid pace through the rubble of Umbertide, one of the larger Italian towns located in the province of Perugia in the north-eastern part of the Umbria region along the course of the southerly flowing Tiber River on 20 June 1944. X Corps moved slowly through the Abruzzi Apennine terrain on an axis of Avezzano-Rieti-Terni-Todi-Perugia. It was not until 10 June that X Corps reached Avezzano, the former site of the German Tenth Army headquarters during the Cassino battles. After unexpected Nazi resistance north of Todi, X Corps' 8th Indian Division moved east onto Spoleto and Trevi and then captured Perugia on 20 June. X Corps was now south of the Albert Line enemy defences abreast with both XIII Corps and US Fifth Army to the west (*NARA*).

(**Above**) An American truck and a towed 203mm Howitzer were first destroyed by a German landmine and then by its own exploding ammunition in Buonconvento, 6 miles to the south-east of Siena and 43 miles south of Florence, on 1 July 1944. As had occurred throughout the Sicilian and southern Italian campaigns, the retreating Nazis expertly sowed roads with mines and demolished structures to impede the Allied advance. (*USAMHI*)

(**Opposite, above**) American soldiers of the 34th Division's 133rd Infantry Regiment inspect a destroyed German Mk VI 'Tiger' tank knocked out by a 75mm armour-piercing (AP) round in Cecina on 2 July 1944. The 34th Division took the place of the 36th Division after the latter was sent back to Naples for the upcoming invasion of southern France. Cecina was defended by the German 16th SS Panzer Grenadier Division, but this unit retreated in the face of the 34th Division's assault on the coastal town. (*USAMHI*)

(**Opposite, below**) An American soldier examines stacked German artillery shells left behind near Volterra on 7 July 1944. The US Fifth Army continued northward inland from the Ligurian coast to the Arno River and Florence. (*USAMHI*)

(**Opposite, above**) Infantrymen from a US 34th Infantry Division's tank destroyer battalion move cautiously up a road after one of their armoured vehicles was destroyed near Castiglioncello on 13 July 1944. (*NARA*)

(**Opposite, below**) Two abandoned German Mk IV Panzers on the road to Pontedera east of the port of Leghorn (Livorno) on 18 July 1944. This area had been defended by the German XIV Corps' 65th Infantry and elements of the 16th SS Panzer Grenadier divisions. (*NARA*)

(**Above**) Part of a squad of Japanese-American soldiers, or *Nisei*, of the 100th Battalion of the 442nd RCT, which was attached to the US 34th Infantry Division, is shown in a captured German VW Type 166 *Schwimmwagen* command and reconnaissance vehicle re-painted with Allied insignia. The 442nd was moving on Leghorn, as part of US IV Corps' advance along the Ligurian coast between Cecina and Pisa. Leghorn was defended by elements of the German XIV Panzer Corps of Lemelsen's Fourteenth Army, but was captured by the Americans on 19 July 1944. (*USAMHI*)

(**Opposite, above**) In Leghorn, US infantrymen of the 34th Division's 135th Regiment are manning a Browning M1917 0.30-inch calibre water-cooled machine-gun. The 91st Division's 363rd Infantry Regiment was attached to the 34th and moved on Leghorn from the east. The Americans met minimal resistance on 19 July 1944, as the Germans had already withdrawn leaving only a weak rear-guard. However, much of Leghorn's port facilities were destroyed by Nazi demolitions. Landmines and booby traps abounded in Leghorn claiming hundreds of American casualties in the weeks after the port's capture. (*NARA*)

(**Above**) American infantrymen pass a sign for Pisa during their Ligurian coast drive to the mouth of the Arno River. On 23 July 1944, two battalions of the US 91st Division's 363rd Regiment, still attached to the near-exhausted 34th Division veterans of Cassino and Anzio, occupied Pisa along the southern bank of the Arno River. With all bridges destroyed, the American infantry dug-in, remote from Pisa's historic monuments, and withstood Nazi artillery and mortar shelling. (*NARA*)

(**Opposite, below**) Soldiers of the US 34th Infantry Division are shown crouching until the road ahead is cleared of German snipers near Cappanoli. A truck with a towed 57mm anti-tank (AT) gun is to the left. After taking Leghorn on 19 July, the 34th Division reached the mouth of the Arno River and the town of Pisa four days later. At this time the elements of 91st Infantry Division were north of Pontedera on the Arno, while to the east the 88th Infantry Division also reached the river. (*USAMHI*)

(**Opposite, above**) Infantrymen of the US 92nd ('Buffalo') Division's 370th Regiment load a 0.30-inch calibre Browning light machine-gun along the Arno River during the advance east from Pisa. Clark had decided against crossing the river immediately so that his formations could pause for reorganisation and resupply. This respite enabled Kesselring to strengthen his defences in the Northern Apennines as well as restore his lines of communication across the Po River via a ferry service as Allied air-raids destroyed the bridges. (*NARA*)

(**Opposite, below**) A British XIII Corps infantry section moves through Montespertoli, 12 miles south-west of Florence, overlooking the Arno River. Alexander attached XIII Corps to become the US Fifth Army's right flank after the FEC divisions were re-deployed in mid-July for the upcoming southern France invasion. The British infantry advance in Montespertoli was assisted by tanks of the 1st Canadian Armoured Brigade attached to XIII Corps. (*NARA*)

(**Above**) A well-camouflaged column of M4 medium tanks of the 1st Canadian Armoured Brigade in Montespertoli. The armour was attached to British XIII Corps to provide tank support and create disinformation for German intelligence officers about the location of Eighth Army's planned attack on the Gothic Line as this Canadian formation was so far to the west of where Operation Olive was to ultimately be launched. (*NARA*)

(**Above**) An M7 105mm Howitzer 'Priest' Gun Motor Carriage of the 1st Canadian Armoured Brigade advances along the Arno River as apart of British XIII Corps advance towards Florence in late July 1944. The 1st Canadian Armoured Brigade was one of only two independent armoured combat brigades from Canada. The brigade landed at Pachino during the Sicilian invasion and crossed over the Strait of Messina to the Italian mainland on 3 September 1943 and fought at Potenza, Termoli, Ortona, and as part of the breakthrough into the Liri Valley in May 1944. (NARA)

(**Opposite**) A British XIII Corps patrol approaches the Arno River and Florence from the east to the north of Arezzo. The mid-span of a bridge over the Arno was destroyed by the retreating Germans. On 15 July, XIII Corps launched its Arezzo offensive against the German Tenth Army's LXXVI Panzer Corps formation. Arezzo was an important rail junction and it fell to the British on the second day of the locale's encirclement from the west. On 16 July, XIII Corps' 8th Indian and 2nd New Zealand divisions veered west towards Florence. To the east, British X Corps advanced towards the Arno in the direction of Bibbiena. (NARA)

(**Opposite, above**) The crew of a Browning M1917 0.30-inch calibre water-cooled machine-gun with a flash suppressor of the US 85th Division's 338th Infantry Regiment fire their weapon in support of advancing infantry on the approaches to Florence along the southern bank of the Arno River in late July 1944. *(USAMHI)*

(**Opposite, below**) A 57mm anti-tank (AT) gun crew of the US 88th Infantry Division, providing covering fire for infantry crossing the Arno River in early August 1944. The gun, patterned on the British 6-pounder, was situated right along the southern bank of the river with a destroyed railroad bridge off to the left. *(NARA)*

(**Above**) British, Indian, New Zealand and South African troops all converged on Florence on 4 August 1944 after Kesselring had declared it an open city on 23 June and ordered his army commanders to remove all but internal security personnel from the city. All the bridges across the Arno were destroyed, with the exception of the renowned Ponte Vecchio, under Hitler's direct orders. Here, British infantrymen march in a single column past the architectural monuments along the Piazza Duomo on 5 August. *(NARA)*

(**Above**) A Universal Carrier of the 6th South African Armoured Division, with cheering Florentines on and around it, moves along a main street. During the night of 3 August, the Imperial Light Horse of the 6th South African Armoured Division entered the southern portion of the city and reached the Arno River the next day. (*USAMHI*)

(**Opposite**) A German propaganda poster on the side of a building in now-liberated Florence claiming that 'The Germans are your friends'. However, it was the British Eighth Army that was viewed as friends. Leese had ceded XIII Corps to a now-depleted Fifth Army, as Clark lost seven divisions to the invasion of southern France. The 8th Indian, 2nd New Zealand, the 6th South African Armoured along with the 1st Canadian Armoured Brigade moved to within 5 miles west of Florence on 22 July 1944. The British 4th Division crossed to the northern side of the Arno 7 miles to the east of Florence. By nightfall of 5 August, XIII Corps was in firm control of the south bank of the Arno from near Empoli eastward to Florence. (*USAMHI*)

LA GERMANIA È VERAMENTE
VOSTRA AMICA

A British military policeman ('Red Cap') nails a warning sign about not making dust, among other precautions, onto a stone wall of a Florentine building from atop his Jeep as an Allied motorised column, including a Churchill Infantry tank, moves along a narrow street. (*NARA*)

A British rifleman in a building on the outskirts of Florence along the southern bank of the Arno River keeps a lookout for any Nazi sniper activity. Kesselring was unable to supply a densely populated Florence, so on 2 August 1944, he abandoned the previously open city. Elements of the German I Parachute Corps, with their backs to the Arno throughout 3 August, covered the withdrawal. Allied artillery fire did hit areas south of the city as well as an occasional large calibre projectile striking some areas within Florence itself. On 4 August, under mounting British XIII Corps pressure, the German parachutist rear-guard withdrew across the Arno both east and west of Florence. (*NARA*)

American artillerymen from Battery C of the 598th Field Artillery of the 92nd ('Buffalo') Division's 370th Infantry Regiment fire their 105mm Howitzers from dug-in gun pits at Casciana Alta across the Arno River in early August 1944. The 92nd Division, along with the 1st, 6th and 11th RCTs of the Brazilian Expeditionary Force, were to gain sufficient combat experience in the US IV Corps sector and give relief to the battle-weary 34th Infantry Division that went into reserve for rest and refitting. Additionally, Task Force (TF) 45 was created to defend a 10-mile defensive zone south of the Gothic Line and was comprised of AA battalions converted into infantry, tank destroyers, tanks and heavy AA artillery, under the command of Brigadier-General Cecil Rutledge, who had formerly commanded the 45th AA Brigade. (NARA)

(**Opposite, above**) A patrol of the US 92nd ('Buffalo') Division's 370th Infantry Regiment takes on German machine-gun nests with bazookas and other small arms fire in early October 1944 to become further combat-tested on the Ligurian coastal flank. Of the three African-American divisions activated during the war, only the 92nd would eventually serve as a complete division. The 370th Regiment, along with the US 2nd Armoured Group, comprised Task Force (TF) 92 and attacked up the Ligurian coast toward Massa. TF 92 was augmented with the 434th and 435th AA battalions, converted into infantry, and supported by the 751st Tank Battalion supported the 849th Tank Destroyer Battalion. (*NARA*)

(**Opposite, below**) American infantrymen and sappers of the 92nd ('Buffalo') Division's 370th Regiment mark-out lanes for M4 medium tanks of the reorganised US 1st Armoured Division to cross the Arno River in August 1944. The 92nd Division had established a bridgehead across the river. (*NARA*)

(**Above**) British infantrymen from the Hampshire Regiment of the 46th Division as part of British V Corps march eastward towards the Adriatic corridor for what was to be the start of Eighth Army's component of Operation Olive, the attack on the German Gothic Line, due to commence on 25 August. (*NARA*)

Chapter Five

Assault on the Gothic Line

By the end of August 1944, the Allies were poised before the Gothic Line defences. Alexander believed that the key to breaking this defensive belt was in the Adriatic sector, especially along the Gemmano-Coriano Ridge complex. Leese argued that if the terrain were attacked in a surprise manner (Operation Olive) by Eighth Army and could then be breached, Allied armour could move through this Adriatic coastal defence zone onto the Romagna Plain to the south of the Po River and secure an area along an east-west axis of Ravenna-Bologna-Modena. This offensive would set up a later thrust towards the Po River and a subsequent move onto an east-west line of Venice-Padua-Verona-Brescia.

Clark's Fifth Army was to make only initial demonstrations against the centre front on the north-south Bologna-Florence axis through the Northern Apennines to coincide with Eighth Army's start of Operation Olive, which began on 25–26 August in the Adriatic sector. Alexander had previously attached British XIII Corps and the 1st Canadian Armoured Brigade to the Fifth Army sector and control to the east of Florence in order to bring it back to operational strength.

Despite the Allied deception of having the 1st Canadian Armoured Brigade along the Fifth Army front, the Nazis recovered a copy of the message sent by Leese to his troops just before Operation Olive commenced. Kesselring moved elements of the German 26th Panzer and 29th Panzer Grenadier divisions along with the 98th Infantry Division from reserve in Bologna to occupy lines north of the Foglia River by 30 August.

The Eighth Army lined-up south of the Gothic Line for Operation Olive over a 30-mile front along the southern bank of the Metauro River, stretching westward from the Adriatic coast north of Ancona with ten divisions dispersed among three Corps, along with 1,200 tanks and 1,000 artillery pieces. Leese was to face Vietinghoff's Tenth Army, situated almost entirely to the north of the Foglia River. The German forces comprised Herr's LXXVI Panzer Corps on the Adriatic coast stretching inland. As of 15 August, Kesselring believed that the US Seventh Army's landing in southern France, Operation Dragoon, precluded any major simultaneous Italian offensive onto the Gothic Line.

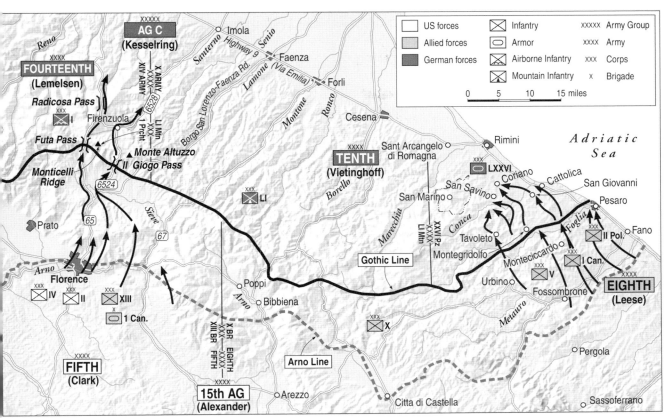

The Gothic Line battles. Two separate campaigns were waged along the Nazi Gothic Line from 25 August to 18 September 1944. Eighth Army's start of Operation Olive began first on 25–26 August in the Adriatic sector with Leese's divisions from the British V, I Canadian and II Polish Corps advancing from north of the Metauro to the Foglia River just south of the German fortifications. Alexander had previously attached British XIII Corps and the 1st Canadian Armoured Brigade to the Fifth Army sector to bring Clark's forces back up to operational strength for the launch of its 10 September attack into the Northern Apennines. The main Fifth Army thrust was in the US II Corps sector with the 34th, 85th and 91st divisions advancing north of Florence along Highway 65 and Road No. 6524 towards Kesselring's Nazi Gothic Line positions guarding the strategic Futa and Il Giogo Passes, the latter situated between the Monticelli Ridge and Monte Altuzzo. US IV Corps mounted a holding attack to keep Germans from reinforcing the Nazi I Parachute Corps. British XIII Corps was to exert pressure on the right and broaden the front towards the Sieve River and Highway 67. (*Philip Schwartzberg, Meridian Mapping*)

The Polish II Corps, on the right flank, covered the Adriatic coast inland for 7 miles. Its two infantry divisions and one armoured brigade were to seize the elevated terrain to Pesaro's north along coast Highway 16.

The I Canadian Corps was on the left of the Poles. It was to attack along a 2-mile front with the British 21st Tank Brigade and the Household Cavalry Regiment attached to its 1st Canadian Division and 5th Canadian Armoured Division.

To the west of the Canadians was Keightley's British V Corps, which had the critical mission to attack and seize approximately 10 miles of elevated terrain between the Metauro and Foglia rivers, the latter just to the south of the Gothic Line's fortifications. Then Keightley's divisions were to break through the northerly running series of ridges from Zollara in the south through an axis of Gemmano-Croce-San Savino-Passano-Coriano. Such an 'opening of the gate' was to enable hundreds of British 1st Armoured Division tanks to move north-westward along the Romagna Plain towards Bologna and then north to the Po River. To the British V Corps' left was the British X Corps, which abutted on Clark's right flank, and was to have no part in the initial attack with its 10th Indian Division and British 9th Armoured Brigade.

Eighth Army commenced their attack on the night of 25 August without a preparatory artillery bombardment to achieve maximum surprise. Also, Vietinghoff, and the German 1st Parachute Division leader, Heidrich, were both away on leave. Infantry divisions crossed the shallow Metauro River unopposed and by the next sunrise were on their way to the Foglia River, which they reached on 29 August. On 30 August, elements of the 4th Indian Division of British V Corps first captured Monte della Croce and then Montecalvo on the Foglia's northern bank amid difficult mountain country. Elements of the British 46th Infantry Division also crossed the Foglia on 30 August to the east of the Indians. By 31 August, the 46th Division's Hampshire Regiment captured the formidable Montegridolfo, while a battalion of the Leicesters seized nearby Mondaino. Stout German defences at the town of Tavoleto, to the west of Mondaino, were attacked by the 2/7th Gurkhas of the 4th Indian Division. This area, laden with minefields and gun positions, was taken by the Gurkha infantry, albeit with heavy casualties, on 1 September.

The I Canadian Corps' attack with elements of two divisions commenced on 25–26 August and by nightfall on the 26th had advanced 5 miles. The Canadians had not attacked in strength and their armour was delayed by Nazi demolitions. On 27 August, the Canadian Corps commander, Burns, and the 1st Canadian Infantry Division's commanding general, Vokes, were both unsure that their forces could first reach the Foglia River on 28 August and then breach the Gothic Line. Despite the loss of many tanks, the Canadians crossed the Foglia late on 30 August. After losing scores of men in a minefield, the Canadians continued to move past Montecchio and Osteria Nuova on the northern side of the river during the late afternoon of 30 August. Now Burns urged Leese that he should attack the Gothic Line immediately as German reinforcements had not concentrated there yet. On 1 September, after losing many tanks to German 88mm AT guns, the Canadians defeated a Nazi force at Tomba di Pesaro and threatened to encircle the rear of the 1st Parachute Division on the coast. The Canadians had broken through the Gothic Line in their attack of 30–31 August and, after capturing San Giovanni on 2 September, they continued their drive to Cattolica located along the Adriatic coast and crossed the Conca River by 3 September as German units of the LXXVI Panzer Corps were hastily pulled back from the pierced Gothic Line in this far eastern sector. The Canadian advance then moved on towards Rimini on the Adriatic coast.

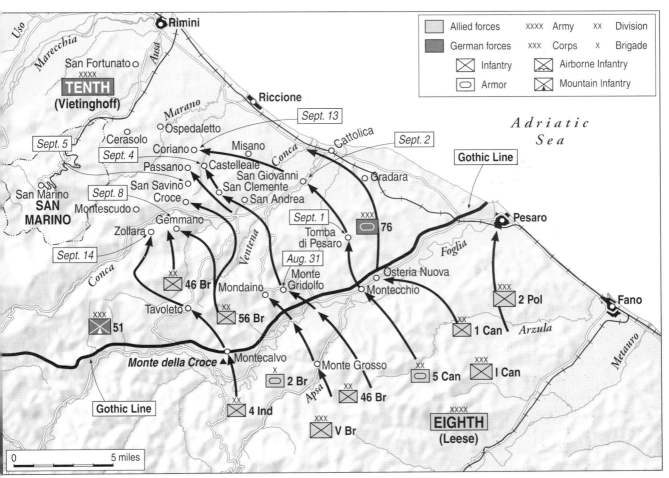

Eighth Army's Gothic Line attack. Without preparatory bombardment, Eighth Army's British V, I Canadian and II Polish Corps crossed the Metauro River on 25–26 August 1944 and reached the Foglia River on 29 August. The next day, 4th Indian Division units captured Monte della Croce and Montecalvo on the Foglia's northern bank. Also, on 30 August, after a Foglia crossing, British 46th Division's Hampshire Regiment pierced the Gothic Line and captured the formidable Monte Gridolfo on 31 August while the Leicesters seized nearby Mondaino. The 4th Indian Division's Gurkha units attacked heavily defended Tavoleto on 31 August, capturing it on 1 September. I Canadian Corps crossed the Foglia on 30 August and moved past Montecchio and Osteria Nuova. The Canadians then seized Tomba di Pesaro on 1 September, losing many tanks to LXXVI Panzer Corps artillery. By 2 September, the Canadians had captured San Giovanni, moved onto Cattolica and crossed the Conca River the next day. Meanwhile, the Poles captured Pesaro and advanced up the Adriatic coastal highway. San Andrea and San Clemente fell to the British 46th Division on 3 September. However, the next day, German stiffened resistance stopped the Hampshire Regiment at Castelleale. On 4–5 September, gruesome combat erupted all along the Coriano Ridge as a 1st British Armoured Division advance was halted at San Savino. On 6–7 September, British 56th Division units briefly took Gemmano before a Nazi 100th Mountain Regiment counter-attack evicted them. On 8 September, the 56th's Queen's Brigade attacked Gemmano, seizing only a fraction. The British 46th Division was committed to the Gemmano assault after crossing the Ventena River. On 9 September, Eighth Army broke through San Savino with heavy tank losses. After days of British V Corps' inability to breach the Coriano-Gemmano Ridge to get into the Marano River Valley, Leese sent I Canadian Corps westward from Riccione to outflank Coriano on 13 September. Canadian infantry took Coriano as British 1st Armoured Division tanks with mounted infantry took Passano. On 14 September, the 4th Indian Division captured Gemmano and Zollara. As Eighth Army moved west of Passano, the Marano River's floodwaters, after previous days of heavy rains, slowed the advance onto the waterlogged Romagna Plain. The 1st Canadian Infantry Division and the 3rd Greek Mountain Brigade captured Rimini on 21 September. (*Philip Schwartzberg, Meridian Mapping*)

Farthest along the Adriatic were the Poles, who inflicted heavy casualties on a German parachute regiment that was caught in the open. The veterans of the Fourth Battle for Cassino had exacted revenge on the Nazi parachutists and now cleared the Eight Army's right flank for the advance.

In the British V Corps sector, units from the British 46th Division seized a bridge across the Ventena River, which paralleled the Conca River to the north. Both waterways had to be crossed for V Corps to manoeuvre towards Coriano at the northern terminus of the Gemmano-Coriano Ridge line in order for British armour to gain entry onto the Romagna Plain. A variety of British regiment battalions captured the successive villages of San Andrea and San Clemente on 3 September. However, the next day a battalion from the Hampshire Regiment was stopped at Castelleale, situated just to the north-west of San Clemente. German resistance was stiffening.

British V Corps headquarters reinforced its 4th Indian Division that had been slowed by the fighting at Tavoleto with elements of the British 56th Division, which attacked and seized Montefiore. However, the latter unit's advance was stopped in gruesome combat at Gemmano and along the Coriano Ridge near Croce on 4 September by well-situated Nazi artillery and mountain troops, and reinforcements dispatched from Bologna. Eighth Army infantry had still to reach the Marano River to the west of the ridgeline in order for the British 1st Armoured Division to move on to the Romagna Plain. Ultimately, a British 1st Armoured Division advance was stopped at San Savino on 5 September. As the British 56th Division had already committed its reserve units to unsuccessfully attack Gemmano on 8–9 September, units from the British 46th Division resumed an attack on San Savino and broke through several days later with the aid of tanks of the British 1st Armoured Division – casualties were high.

In a tactical shift, Eighth Army headquarters directed an outflanking attack of the Coriano Ridge positions to get into the Marano Valley by driving on Gemmano and Croce in a direct westward movement from just north of Riccione on Highway 16, with a set-piece attack utilising massed artillery and I Canadian Corps, commencing on 13 September. The Canadian 11th Infantry Brigade took Coriano as British 1st Armoured Division tanks with mounted infantry units from the British 4th Division took Passano to the south. As the tanks and infantry moved west from Passano, their advance was curtailed by floodwaters from the Marano River after previous days' heavy rains. Finally, elements of the 4th Indian Division captured Gemmano on 14 September in the midst of a German evacuation of the town.

By the time Rimini on the Adriatic coast, the gateway to the Romagna Plain, had fallen on 21 September to Canadian infantry and Greek Mountain Brigade units, Eighth Army lost almost 15,000 casualties of all types along with 200 tanks. The 2nd New Zealand Division, released from Eighth Army reserve, was now tasked with pursuing the retreating Germans and was referred to as a *corps de chasse* after the fall of Rimini. Kesselring had moved his Tenth Army divisions behind the Marecchia River.

The New Zealanders crossed this river on 22 September and inflicted numerous casualties on the German 162nd Turkoman Division, recruited from expatriate Soviet troops. However, on 24 September, the 2nd New Zealand Division was repulsed by the German 1st Parachute Division. German losses were also staggering and, like the British, the Nazis had numerous understrength infantry units after the almost-four weeks of conflict.

As for the US Fifth Army (with attached British XIII Corps) assault on the Gothic Line, it was drawn-up in line along the Arno River, with IV Corps from the river's mouth to the west of Florence. US IV Corps was situated on the Ligurian coast and extended to 5 miles west of Florence. Crittenberger's IV Corps consisted of the US 1st Armoured and 92nd divisions, Task Force 45, the newly arrived Brazilian Expeditionary Force and the 6th South African Armoured Division (detached from British XIII Corps).

The US II Corps had been concentrated behind Florence in the Fifth Army's centre on a 5-mile front at the end of August and comprised the veteran US 34th, 85th and 88th Infantry divisions as well as the recently arrived 91st Infantry Division. In Keyes' II Corps sector, Highway 65 headed north through the Futa and Radicosa Passes amid the Northern Apennines towards Bologna. A secondary road, No. 6524, which branched off Highway 65 south of San Pietro to the east, led to the naturally stronger II Giogo Pass, which was dominated by two high peaks, Monticelli and Monte Altuzzo, before its continuation through the mountain pass to Firenzuola.

On the Fifth Army's right was Kirkman's British XIII Corps, comprising the British 1st and Indian 8th Infantry and British 6th Armoured divisions, as well as the 1st Canadian Armoured Brigade. XIII Corps, situated to the right of US II Corps, was to use secondary mountain routes, such as Road No. 6528, which emanated from Firenzuola through the Northern Apennines to Imola, located on Highway 9. This highway, also called the Via Emilia, ran from Rimini on the Adriatic coast along a north-westward axis of Cesena-Forli-Faenza-Imola to Bologna and Modena.

Fifth Army's left and centre faced Lemelsen's Fourteenth Army, comprising Senger und Etterlin's depleted XIV Panzer Corps of the 16th *Waffen* SS Panzer Grenadier and the 65th Infantry divisions facing US IV Corps. In the vital centre area, covering the approach routes to Bologna, and opposite US II Corps, was General Ernst Schlemm's I Parachute Corps made up of the 362nd, 4th Parachute and 356th Infantry divisions. The British XIII Corps faced from west to east the 715th, the 334th and the 305th Infantry divisions, part of the right wing of the German Tenth Army under the LI Mountain Corps. All these Nazi formations occupied the forward or outpost zone of the Gothic Line, with main defences that ran eastwards from a point on the coast south of La Spezia along the forward slopes of the Northern Apennines to cover the Futa and II Giogo Passes and then into the LI Mountain Corps sector.

Clark was to have IV Corps mount a holding attack to keep German XIV Panzer Corps from reinforcing the centre while II Corps was to mount the major assault. British XIII Corps was to exert pressure on the right and broaden the front of the II Corps attack. Fifth Army's main attack as part of Operation Olive was not to be launched until 10 September after moving through about 5 miles of German outposts all along its front. On 11 September, the US II and British XIII Corps advanced between Highway 65 and the Sieve River. Eighth Army's earlier attacks to the east succeeded in diverting most enemy units away from the Futa and Il Giogo Passes except for the 10th, 11th and 12th Parachute regiments of the I Parachute Corps' 4th Parachute Division.

The veteran US 34th Division was directed to the enemy's heavily fortified Futa Pass as a feint to convince the Nazis that this was the main American objective. The US 91st Division, under Major-General William G. Livesay, had joined the Fifth Army in July 1944. With the US 85th Division, the 91st was to make the initial assault on the Il Giogo Pass and nearby 3,000-foot Monticelli Ridge and Monte Altuzzo on 12 September. Allied intelligence was wrong and the Il Giogo Pass was defended by the heavily armed 12th Parachute Regiment and the American attack was too dispersed. However, the Il Giogo Pass was also the boundary between the German Tenth and Fourteenth armies, which added to confusion among the Nazi command structure. After difficulties with the assault and a high rate of American casualties, Monticelli Ridge finally fell to the 91st Division's 363rd Infantry Regiment on 18 September. Monte Altuzzo fell shortly thereafter to the 85th Division's 338th Infantry Regiment, but at more than a sixty percent casualty rate in the six days of combat.

The Gothic Line was broken by Fifth Army, but at a steep price in bloodshed. Over 2,100 casualties were incurred by the three 88th Division infantry regiments alone. Like the Eighth Army, Fifth Army was strong in armour but remained weak in infantry now further compounded by the recent losses.

British XIII Corps started its advance on to the Gothic Line on 13 September with the British 1st Division supported by some Canadian tanks of the Ontario Regiment to advance up the Borgo San Lorenzo-Faenza Road. The 1st Division's 66th Brigade attacked the German 715th Infantry Division and took Monte Prefetto, one of the forward Gothic Line positions. The 8th Indian Division advanced with a tank squadron from the Calgary Regiment over trackless ground between the Borgo San Lorenzo-Faenza Road and Highway 67. The British 6th Armoured Division moved up Highway 67 towards Forli situated far to the north-east on Highway 9 along the southern end of the Romagna Plain. By 15 September, both infantry divisions were through the fortifications of the German 715th Infantry Division. Over the ensuing nine days, many locales into the Northern Apennines were seized by the Britons, Gurkhas and Mahrattas of Kirkman's XIII Corps.

A Churchill Infantry tank stirs up road dust as it supports 1st Canadian Infantry Division soldiers north of the Foglia River near Osteria Nuova before the Gothic Line was reached at the end of August 1944. This tank was rushed into production and did poorly during the Dieppe Raid of August 1942. However, it fared better in the rugged Tunisian terrain in the spring of 1943. Now the Churchill and its specialised variants, including the Crocodile flamethrower and a bridge-laying two-tiered armoured vehicle, were to provide important roles across the Gothic Line and the Romagna Plain, the latter with its numerous rivers. (NARA)

Infantrymen of the 2/5th Battalion Leicestershire Regiment of the British 46th Division, manning the British V Corps' right, crouch along a ridge before advancing against Nazi defences near Coldazzo on 2 September 1944. A line of M4 medium tanks is lined up to provide gunfire support. (*NARA*)

(**Opposite, above**) The British V Corps' Hampshire Regiment of the 46th Infantry Division moves up to its assault position for the Gothic Line attack, Operation Olive, which commenced on 25 August 1944. The 5th Battalion of the Hampshire Regiment attacked thick German Tenth Army defences situated on three steep peaks rising up to 1,500 feet. These British 46th Division infantrymen took all three heights with grenades and bayonets by 27 August. (*NARA*)

(**Opposite, below**) A Gurkha Bren gun team of the 4th Indian Infantry Division fights in the rubble of Tavoleto on 1 September 1944 across the Gothic Line defences manned by elements of the German LXXVI Panzer Corps. The 4th Indian Division manned the left flank of the British V Corps' attack during the opening phase of Operation Olive. Tavoleto had to be seized to place the two British V Corps assaulting infantry divisions, along with its reserve infantry and armoured formations, in position to attack the Gemmano-Coriano Ridge complex in an attempt to reach the Marano River. (*NARA*)

(**Opposite, above**) A British V Corps' 46th Infantry Division's 17-pounder AT gun fires at the enemy in Gemmano to the north of Tavoleto on 9 September 1944. The Battle for Gemmano was referred to as the 'Cassino of the Adriatic', involving the British 46th, 56th and 4th Indian divisions from 4–15 September in more than a dozen separate attacks. (*NARA*)

(**Above**) A Canadian infantry patrol advances along a ridge to reconnoitre hidden enemy positions as Allied artillery shells are shown exploding on the far ridge (*background*). On 25 August, Operation Olive opened with the I Canadian Corps advancing along the coastal plain to the left of the II Polish Corps' attack up the Adriatic coast to Pesaro. On 28 August, Kesselring, after reviewing captured Eighth Army orders, knew that this was not a diversionary attack and moved three German divisions from Bologna to this sector. (*NARA*)

(**Opposite, below**) A Canadian 1st Infantry Division sergeant peers into a Nazi outpost in the vicinity of San Giovanni on the Ventena River. The Canadians attacked San Giovanni on 2 September 1944, and due to limited German defence units, they were able to move through the enemy positions towards the Conca River running parallel beyond the Ventena. As the German LXXVI Panzer Corps withdrew behind the Conca River, Heidrich's 1st Parachute Division halted the Canadian advance towards the Marano River at Coriano. (*NARA*)

Canadian infantrymen move past 5th Canadian Armoured Division tanks and crewmen reviewing maps. Infantry-tank co-operation was paramount with armoured units requiring additional infantrymen to seize surrounding heights. The British 1st Armoured Division, using desert tactics in the Gemmano-Coriano Ridge attacks, lost many tanks by not incorporating sufficient infantry. (NARA)

A British V Corps' 46th Infantry Division's Bren gun team from the 6th Yorkshire and Lancashire Regiment covers advancing infantrymen from a shell crater along the side of a ruined street in San Clemente north of the Conca River on 3 September 1944. German defences on the Coriano Ridge were initially too stout for the British V Corps divisions. The village of Croce had changed hands five times in the British attempts to seize the locale. (NARA)

A British Universal Carrier advances past the village of Fuetano and on towards the Republic of San Marino, which is situated due west of the Gemmano-Coriano Ridge, in mid-September 1944. This sector of the Adriatic had undulating high ridges and intervening valleys through which the Gemmano-Coriano Ridge battle was fought. By 17 September, Eighth Army had reached the eastern edge of the neutral Italian republic. (NARA)

(**Above**) In the US Fifth Army sector, high waters of the Arno River threaten to wash out a portion of a pontoon bridge on 8 September 1944. The demolished concrete bridge across the river is shown at Pontedera, which was to be a crossing point for the US 1st Armoured Division. (*USAMHI*)

(**Opposite**) American infantrymen of the 3rd Battalion from the 85th Division's 339th Regiment march in a single column near St. Verruga with the initial Nazi defence line in the background on 18 September 1944. Clark planned to open the Fifth Army phase of Operation Olive on 10 September with his three corps, the US IV, US II and British XIII Corps. The Gothic Line's Futa and II Giogo Passes were to be II Corps' main objectives. (*USAMHI*)

(**Opposite, above**) Infantrymen of the 91st Division, part of US II Corps that was concentrated on a narrow 5-mile front near Florence for Operation Olive, march through Italian vineyards with full packs near Highway 65 on 10 September 1944. After a diversionary attack was made at the Futa Pass by the US 34th Division, the 91st Division, supported by the 85th Division, was to attack the Il Giogo Pass on Road No. 6524, which ran through the boundary of the German Fourteenth and Tenth armies. (*NARA*)

(**Opposite, below**) Infantrymen of the US 92nd ('Buffalo') Division's 370th Regiment march up a steep hill near Casciana Alta in Pisa Province on 11 September 1944. The 370th Infantry, along with the 92nd's 598th Field Artillery Battalion, was part of a polyglot *ad hoc* force that included the three regiments of the Brazilian Expeditionary Force and some Italian partisans. Their task was to acquire combat experience while relieving some battle-weary divisions, such as the 34th Infantry. (*NARA*)

(**Above**) Two American infantrymen from the US 88th Division pass German corpses killed by phosphorus artillery shell bursts on the route north along Road No. 6528 towards Imola. The infantry was supported by units of the US 1st Armoured Division's Combat Command A. (*NARA*)

(**Opposite, above**) A US 85th Division aid station in a captured farmhouse near Monte Altuzzo on 20 September 1944. Monte Altuzzo was part of the Gothic Line's fortifications near the Il Giogo Pass to the south-east of Firenzuola. This area was defended by the German 362nd Infantry Division of the Fourteenth Army's I Parachute Corps and was also near the boundary of the German Fourteenth and Tenth armies, an intended target of Clark's. (*USAMHI*)

(**Above**) British sappers clear debris from a mountain road bridge so that a motorised column of British 1st Division can pass over in the Northern Apennines on 12 September 1944. The bridge crossed the Sieve River, a tributary of the Arno River, the former waterway originating in the Futa Pass area of the mountains. The British 1st Division, as part of British XIII Corps' attachment to Fifth Army, was situated on the US 85th Division's right. (*NARA*)

(**Opposite, below**) An infantry section of the Canadian 1st Division patrols Rimini, the Adriatic port, which was captured after hard fighting by this Eighth Army unit on 21 September 1944. The 3rd Greek Mountain Brigade also participated in the capture after the Germans initiated their withdrawal. (*NARA*)

Infantrymen from the II Polish Corps patrol a town as their unit pursued the retreating German Tenth Army soldiers from Rimini along the Adriatic coast on 23 September 1944. The Polish divisions were to go into Eighth Army reserve prior to General McCreery, the new army commander, having moved the rested 3rd Carpathian and 5th Kresowa Infantry divisions to the left wing of the army south of Highway 9 in mid-October. (*NARA*)

Chapter Six

Advance and Stalemate in the Northern Apennines

Battle of the Rivers

On 22 September 1944, the 2nd New Zealand Division moved from Eighth Army reserve through the 1st Canadian Infantry Division across the Marecchia River against heavy opposition from the German 162nd Turkoman and 1st Parachute divisions. With British, Indian and Canadian divisions, the New Zealanders were to continue a north-westward, hard-fought advance across a series of Nazi-defended rivers: the Fontanaccia; the Uso; and the Fiumicino. These waterways run parallel to one another with their mouths on the Adriatic coast north of Rimini. This Eighth Army series of river assaults lasted until early October. Although the Eighth Army formations compelled the German LXXVI Panzer Corps' 20th *Luftwaffe* Field, 100th Mountain, 114th Jaeger and 90th Panzer Grenadier divisions to retreat in good order, the Nazi-imposed delay, coupled with the arrival of autumn's torrential rains, stalled the Allied advance. To the rear, supply and reinforcement transit across the previously shallow but now 12-foot high raging Marecchia River, flooded by intense rains from 21–28 September, impeded Royal Engineer bridging attempts.

It was not until 26 September that *Staghorn* armoured cars of the New Zealand Divisional Cavalry reached the south bank of the Uso River, near Bellaria, which some contend is the ancient Rubicon site of Caesar's crossing in 49BC. The 5th Canadian Armoured Division, after four days of heavy fighting, seized a bridgehead across the narrow Uso River to the south-west on 25 September. The Canadians had lost 350 tanks since the fall of Rimini four days earlier.

The British 1st Armoured Division, along with some Gurkha units, took Sant Arcangelo di Romagna and crossed the Uso, just beyond on 25 September, while the British 56th Division pushed up Highway 9 and reached Savignano on the south bank of the Fiumicino River by 27 September. Amid the more difficult country of the Northern Apennine foothills, the 4th Indian Division made slow progress and only a few of their troops crossed the Fiumicino at the locale of the same name on the 28 September.

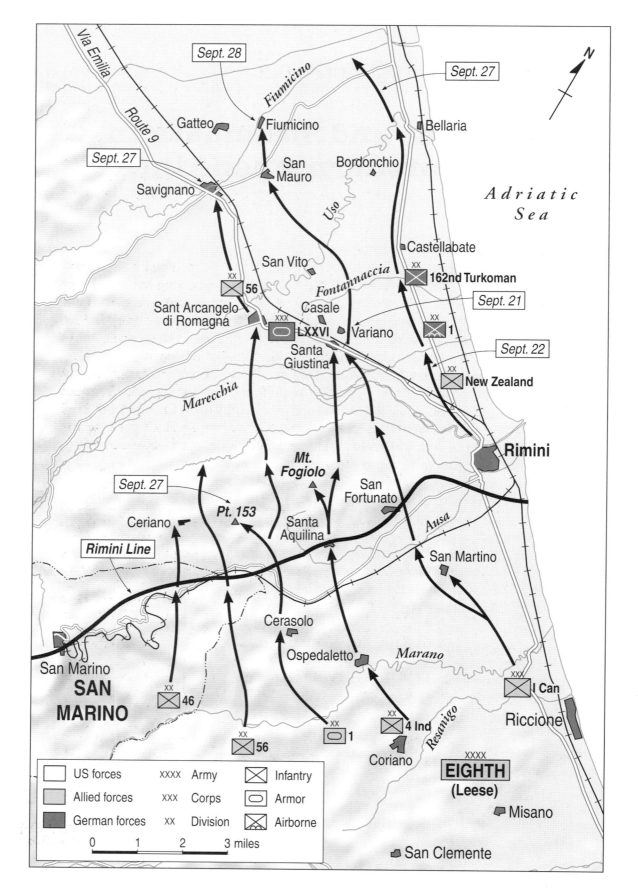

Via Emilia

Route 9

Sept. 28

Fiumicino

Sept. 27

Gatteo

Fiumicino

Bellaria

Sept. 27

San Mauro

Bordonchio

*A d r i a t i c
S e a*

Savignano

San Vito

Uso

Castellabate

XX
162nd Turkoman

San Vito

Fontannaccia

Sant Arcangelo
di Romagna

XX
56

XXX
LXXVI

Casale

Santa
Giustina

Variano

Sept. 21

XX
1

Sept. 22

XX
New Zealand

Marecchia

Rimini

*Mt.
Fogiolo*

Sept. 27

Ceriano

Pt. 153

Santa
Aquilina

San
Fortunato

Ausa

Rimini Line

San Martino

Cerasolo

Marano

Ospedaletto

XX
46

XX
56

XX
1

XX
4 Ind

XXX
I Can

Resanigo

San Marino
**SAN
MARINO**

Coriano

Riccione

EIGHTH
(Leese)

US forces	XXXX	Army	⊠	Infantry
Allied forces	XXX	Corps	⬭	Armor
German forces	XX	Division	⊠	Airborne

0   1   2   3 miles

🚩 Misano

🚩 San Clemente

N

The near-constant rain intensified from 29 September to 2 October. Every ford across the Marecchia and Uso rivers was impassable and the Adriatic sector's terrain north of Rimini was mired in mud, which halted the movement of Eighth Army armoured and motorised columns. Also, Leese's divisions were to become entangled amid strong German defensive works situated on successive ridges to the north-west of Rimini. The German Tenth Army turned to fight for the Fiumicino River forcing a major Eighth Army assault to cross it. Meanwhile, as Kesselring observed the flood-soaked terrain, he transferred units to combat the Northern Apennine sector to confront the Fifth Army.

Combat along the Romagna Plain

Another set of parallel-flowing rivers emanating from the Northern Apennines and emptying into the Adriatic Sea were crossed by Eighth Army during the autumn of 1944, including the Savio, Ronco, Montone and Lamone, before another winter stalemate ensued. More than three weeks transpired after the capture of Sant Arcangelo di Romagna before Indian contingents, together with another British V Corps division, the 46th, reached Cesena on 20 October on Highway 9.

British V Corps attacked towards Forli while II Polish Corps on its left moved towards the high ground south-west of Faenza. After heavy fighting, the Germans withdrew behind the line of the Montone River and Eighth Army units entered Forli on 9 November. The Polish 3rd Carpathian Division reached a point 6 miles to the south of Faenza on 21 November, despite strong German counter-attacks by Herr's LXXVI Panzer Corps, which still covered Highway 9.

Battle of the Rivers. On 22 September 1944, the 2nd New Zealand Division passed through the 1st Canadian Infantry Division in Rimini and trekked across the shallow Marecchia River north-westwards along the Adriatic coast in pursuit of the German LXXVI Panzer Corps. However, the New Zealanders soon met heavy opposition from the Nazi 1st Parachute Division. The 5th Canadian Armoured Division, after four days of heavy fighting with 350 tanks lost, seized a bridgehead on 25 September across the narrow Uso, a small river that empties into the Adriatic near Bellaria to Rimini's north. The next day, New Zealand armoured cars reached the south bank of the Uso. Movement across the Romagna Plain for Eighth Army's divisions was hindered by flooded ground produced due to torrential rains that commenced on 21 September and continued into October. Further delaying the advance was the rising Marecchia in Eighth Army's rear echelon, making supply and reinforcement difficult, while halting motorised columns. Other rivers in the Uso's vicinity were the Fiumicino and the Fontannaccia. The British 1st Armoured Division took Sant Arcangelo di Romagna and crossed the Uso just beyond on 25 September, while the British 56th Division pushed up Highway 9 and reached Savignano on the south bank of the Fiumicino by 27 September. Farther west in the more difficult country of the Northern Apennine foothills, the 4th Indian and British 46th divisions made slow progress and only a few troops crossed the Fiumicino on the 26th. *(Philip Schwartzberg, Meridian Mapping)*

On 25 November, Eighth Army divisions pulled up to the Lamone River outside Faenza on a broad front comprising the Polish 3rd Carpathian, the 10th Indian, the British 46th and the 2nd New Zealand. Heavy rain cancelled air support for any immediate assault for a few days on Faenza, an ancient Italian ceramic centre with fifteenth-century outer walls. British V Corps Commander Keightley isolated Faenza by cutting Highway 9 from the south and east. To the north of Faenza in the British 56th Division sector on the Romagna Plain, the front was relatively quiet.

On the night of 3–4 December, the British 46th and Polish 3rd Carpathian divisions launched a joint attack across the Lamone River in the area south of Highway 9, securing a bridgehead by 7 December against stiffening German resistance. By 13 December, the 2nd New Zealand Division had built a bridge to support a regiment of tanks to cross the Lamone River. The next day, the 10th Indian and the 2nd New Zealand divisions moved into bridgeheads across the river as the Indian troops arrived in time to thwart a strong Nazi counter-attack. Faenza still remained in German control.

On Alexander's orders, the resupplied I Canadian Corps' 5th Armoured Division, under Major-General B.M. Hoffmeister, opened its attack on the night of 2–3 December against Ravenna to Faenza's north-east. The Canadians, occupying the Eighth Army's right wing, entered Ravenna by midday on 4 December amid a partisan uprising. By 6 December, the Canadians also reached another sector on the Lamone River along a 5-mile front to the north-west of Ravenna. Four days later a surprise attack by the Canadian 5th Armoured and elements of the 1st Infantry divisions, without artillery support, made good progress forcing a crossing over the lower reaches of the Lamone River and started to build bridges.

British V Corps launched its assault on Faenza during the night of 14 December with more than 400 artillery pieces supporting the advance of the 2nd New Zealand Division from the south-west and the 10th Indian Division from the east of the city. On the V Corps' left flank, the II Polish Corps troops, on the night of 14–15 December, closed up to the Senio River, 2 miles to the west, to outflank Faenza still defended by dwindling cadres of the German 90th Panzer Grenadier and 26th Panzer divisions. The Nazis began to withdraw to the north-west to establish themselves on the Senio River, 3 miles away, to avoid encirclement. The 10th Indian Division's 43rd Motorised Gurkha Infantry Brigade rolled into parts of Faenza on 15–16 December and the next day established two small bridgeheads west of Faenza on the Senio. The 2nd New Zealand Division also reached the Senio on 16 December. The Germans withdrew entirely by 22 December.

The German XIV Panzer Corps commander, Senger und Etterlin, relieved the 26th Panzer Division's remnant force with the 29th Panzer Grenadier Division as part of three divisions he had dispatched from the Northern Apennines front to oppose the Eighth Army's solitary thrust for the Senio River and beyond to the Santerno, 11 miles to the west, the latter running through Imola on Highway 9. On the night of 19–20 December, the British 56th Division resumed its attack north from Faenza and, after linking up with the Canadians on 21 December, had cleared the eastern bank of the Senio River by 6 January. McCreery's Eighth Army was situated across the Lamone River to the Senio, both tributaries of the winding Reno River. After having fought steadily increasing enemy reinforcements, exacerbating manpower and artillery ammunition shortages, the bulk of Eighth Army was to remain on the Senio River until the spring offensive in April 1945. The onset of adverse weather and mounting casualty lists imposed another winter's stalemate on the Italian campaign in 1944–45.

The Canadians continued to move forward to the south of Lake Comacchio in early January in preparation for the spring assault on the Argenta Gap in mid-April. During the combat along the Romagna Plain, the I Canadian Corps alone incurred well over 2,000 casualties with more than 500 killed, 1,800 wounded and 200 missing in action. As manpower shortages in north-west Europe in Montgomery's 21st Army Group were mounting, the I Canadian Corps' two divisions were withdrawn from Italy in early 1945 for redeployment with General Harold Crerar's First Canadian Army in Holland.

The German withdrawal from Greece in autumn 1944 was indirectly to further compound the Eighth Army's manpower shortages. Greece was plunged into a civil war between the ELAS communist guerrillas and the Greek Royal Army, who supported the king. Churchill elected to support the Royal Army and the Greek government with supplies initially and then with troops. The Greek Mountain Brigade left Eighth Army at the end of October and it was followed in December by the British 4th and 46th Infantry and 4th Indian divisions, which were dispatched to Athens by Field Marshal Wilson.

Fifth Army assaults into the Northern Apennines

The combination of autumn rain, which swelled streams, washed out bridges and obscured visibility, along with the Nazis' expert tactics at delaying with road demolitions and landmines, made progress extremely slow. From 22 September until the end of the month, US II Corps' divisions had advanced less than 10 miles.

As part of this advance, on 24 September 1944, Clark redirected US II Corps' 34th, 85th and 91st Infantry divisions towards Bologna via the Radicosa Pass on Highway 65 north of the Futa Pass. The II Corps forces also moved onto Firenzuola north of the Il Giogo Pass via road No. 6524. The US 88th Division vectored towards Imola on Highway 9 via the mountain road No. 6528 veering to the north-east, which was intended to trap the German Tenth Army between the two Allied armies.

Despite Kesselring reinforcing his positions in front of Clark's Fifth Army, elements of the US 88th Division seized the 2,400-foot high Monte Battaglia on 25 September along road No. 6528 toward Imola. Elements of four new Nazi divisions were brought into the area to halt the Fifth Army drive for Imola. The 6th South African Armoured Division and CCB of the US 1st Armoured Division covered Fifth Army's left flank, while the British 78th Infantry Division was transferred to British XIII Corps from Eighth Army to support Clark's right flank. Further to the west, the German Fourteenth Army also retreated into the Northern Apennines behind the pierced Gothic Line to delay the US IV Corps divisions.

Beginning on 1 October 1944, US II Corps trekked 4 miles in three days amid the harsh terrain along Highway 65 and by 2 October reached Monghidoro, only a score of miles from Bologna. Stiff German defence again materialised. The US 91st Infantry Division suffered 1,700 casualties during the first four days of October. During the next week's combat between 5–9 October, Fifth Army incurred another 1,400 casualties for a gain of a few more miles. Kesselring was still adept at shifting his forces around from the less active Ligurian Sea front against US IV Corps to combat local threats made by the US II Corps advance.

The third US II Corps push began on 10 October against the Livergnano Escarpment, the strongest Nazi terrain position in the Northern Apennines. The ground was manned by the German 4th Parachute, 94th, 362nd and now 65th Infantry divisions. On 16 October, the US 34th Division attempted to break through to Bologna but the attack was quickly stopped. The 337th Infantry Regiment of the US 85th Division, leading the II Corps attack through thick mud, reached Monte Grande, but was stopped by Nazi machine-gun positions on 20 October only 4 miles from Highway 9. The British 78th Division on Fifth Army's right stormed Monte Spaduro on 23 October, but the Nazis held their positions.

The US II Corps advance north of Florence into the Northern Apennines was halted 10 miles south of Bologna. Kesselring had obeyed Hitler's directive to continue resistance south of the Po River. Since the start of the US II Corps offensive in Operation Olive on 10 September, Keyes' four American divisions had lost more than 15,000 men killed or wounded. On 26 October, torrential rain washed out bridges, cutting Fifth Army's lines of communications (LOC). Thus, on 28 October, without adequate infantry replacements and with supply lines threatened, Keyes ordered all of his divisions to go on to the defensive while falling back on more easily sustainable positions. Another winter's stalemate was approaching in the Northern Apennines south of Bologna as well as east of the city along the Romagna Plain.

General Truscott returned to Italy from southern France on 15 December 1944 to command Fifth Army just as the Germans were heavily reinforcing their front opposite US IV Corps on the Ligurian coast in the vicinity of the Serchio River valley. With a combination of SS Panzer, Mountain, regular infantry and Italian fascist forces, the Nazis launched Operation *Wintergewitter* on 26 December against the US 92nd Division to the north of Lucca. US IV Corps commander Crittenberger quickly moved elements of the US 1st Armoured, US 34th Infantry and 8th Indian divisions to staunch the hole in the 'Buffalo' division's lines near Barga and, after four days of heavy fighting, compelled the Nazis and Italian fascists to withdraw.

By early January 1945, the German and Allied armies, amid deep snowfall as well as infantry and ammunition shortfalls, made winter lines along the Senio River, stretching across Highway 9 to Imola's south-east. The Germans were dug-in deeply along the far flood-bank, several feet in height with numerous weapons pits. The Eighth Army veterans were holding the near bank. Alexander had been directed to contain the Germans in Italy and prevent their withdrawal to other fronts. One exasperated American colonel in the Northern Apennines exclaimed, 'You can't fight a goddam battle unless you have the goddam troops'. The Allies were to prepare for a new offensive aimed at the Po Valley and Bologna in early April.

Prior to the spring offensive, two inexperienced American infantry regiments, the 365th and 366th, of the US 92nd Division failed, with high casualties over four days of combat, in early February to push back the Italian fascist units in the Serchio River valley near Massa and the Cinquale Canal in US IV Corps. The US 10th Mountain Division, which arrived on the front on 27 December, attacked on 19 February to secure exits from the Northern Apennines directly into the Po Valley at such locales as Monte Belvedere and Monte della Torraccia. By 5 March, the accomplishments of the 10th Mountain Division had secured the heights for the Allied spring offensive.

In late March, the Japanese-American *Nisei* 442nd RCT returned from southern France. After the failed US 92nd Division attack on Massa and the Cinquale Canal in February 1945, General Marshall reorganised the 'Buffalo' Division for the upcoming spring Allied thrust. The best troops from the 365th and 371st Infantry regiments joined the skilled 370th Regiment. This fragmented division was then assigned the US 473rd Infantry Regiment, an all-white unit, and the 442nd Japanese-American *Nisei* 442nd RCT. This created the US Army's only division integrated down to the regimental level.

(**Above**) Two New Zealand 19th Armoured Brigade's M4 medium tanks in Rimini during the last week of September 1944 after the Canadians and the Greek Mountain Brigade captured the port-city. Alexander unleashed Freyberg's 2nd New Zealand Division to pursue the Germans across the several parallel-running rivers, the Marecchia, Fontannaccia, Uso and Fiumicino, all emptying into the Adriatic, to capture Ravenna and emerge onto the Romagna Plain, for a drive along Highway 9 towards Bologna. (*NARA*)

(**Opposite**) British V Corps troops in late September, during the Battle of the Rivers, provide covering fire for advancing troops across a bank of the Uso River near Bellaria, 22 miles south of Ravenna. The Uso River is a shallow river that flows from the Northern Apennine Mountains to the Adriatic Sea through the south-eastern end of the Romagna Plain near Sant Arcangelo di Romagna. (*NARA*)

(**Opposite, above**) A Gurkha Vickers 0.303-inch calibre water-cooled machine-gun position in the bedroom of a ruined house in Sant Arcangelo di Romagna to the west of Rimini on Highway 9 on the Romagna Plain, at the end of September 1944. (*NARA*)

(**Opposite, below**) A Universal Carrier of British V Corps about to cross a bridge over one of the rivers south of Ravenna in late September 1944 during the Battle of the Rivers campaign for 2nd New Zealand Division. The Nazi LXXVI Panzer Corps units skilfully withdrew to defend the next river, delaying the British V Corps entry into Cesena until 20 October. (*NARA*)

(**Above**) An infantry column from the British 56th Division's Queen's Royal Regiment crosses what may have been the ancient shallow Rubicon that Caesar traversed in 49BC. The area between the white tape markers had been cleared of landmines by sappers. The movement across the many rivers of the rain-flooded Romagna Plain exhausted McCreery's Eighth Army's corps. The end of October 1944 was marked by a near-standstill of these formations across a 30-mile front, extending from the Adriatic coast 8 miles to Ravenna's south to the vicinity of Forli along Highway 9 on the Montone River, 10 miles to Faenza's south-east. (*NARA*)

(**Opposite, above**) A British truck column attempts to cross surging floodwaters and mud along the Romagna Plain north of Highway 9 in the drive towards Cesena during the last week of October 1944. McCreery, Eighth Army commander since 1 October, shifted his advance to the foothills of the Northern Apennines, south of Highway 9, which offered better operational terrain than the waterlogged plain and flooded rivers of the Romagna north of the highway. For the north-westward advance towards Bologna, the II Polish Corps shifted along better-drained terrain south of the highway. The British V Corps' 10th Indian and British 46th and 56th Infantry divisions continued their north-westward advance along the axis of Cesena-Forli-Faenza-Imola, while the I Canadian Corps held the remainder of the Eighth Army's front from Highway 9 to the coast, 7 miles to the north-east. (*NARA*)

(**Above**) British 46th Division infantrymen enter Cesena on 20 October 1944. The German resistance was stout until 17 October, when elements of the Nazi LXXVI Panzer Corps began withdrawing to the far bank of the Savio River. As Nazi forces in Cesena thinned, the 46th Division's pace into Cesena quickened. British V Corps units crossed the Savio River on the night of 22–23 October. After the Savio's crossing, the 2nd New Zealand Division went into Eighth Army reserve, having incurred more than 2,000 casualties, many contracting hepatitis. (*NARA*)

(**Opposite, below**) Royal Artillery gunners ignite smoke canisters to obscure bridging efforts along the Savio River's east bank just beyond Cesena in late October 1944. The British 4th Division relieved the 46th for the river assault. However, long-range enemy artillery delayed bridge construction until 23 October, which enabled the 4th Division's crossing south of Cesena to begin the advance towards the Ronco River, 9 miles to the north-west. (*NARA*)

(**Above**) Gurkha infantrymen of the 10th Indian Division hold on to guide ropes to assist their fording of the Ronco River between Cesena and Forli. After crossing the Savio River on 23 October, the Gurkhas swung north-west to arrive along the Ronco, which flows north of Forli on the Romagna Plain where it joins the Montone River south of Ravenna. These soldiers from the 10th Indian Division were able to cross the Ronco on 26 October and widen their bridgehead, which compelled to the Nazis to retreat from this area to Forli's south four days later. (*NARA*)

(**Opposite, above**) A 40mm Bofors anti-aircraft (AA) gun crew from the 6th South African Armoured Division's 28th Regiment, on 1 November 1944 along the eastern bank of the Reno River, as the waterway originated in the Northern Apennines to the west of the Futa Pass and meandered to the west of Bologna and then north along the Romagna Plain through Argenta. The AA gun crew, utilising the weapon in a direct fire support role, waited for the dense morning fog to lift for better observation. The 6th South African Armoured Division comprised Fifth Army's right flank of US IV Corps' sector. (*NARA*)

(**Opposite, below**) Members of a machine-gun section from the 10th Indian Division move with their pack mule through Meldola on 2 November after crossing the Ronco River. The Indians had made it halfway to Forli, situated on Highway 9, which the British 4th and 46th Infantry divisions entered on 9 November 1944. Occupation of Forli by British V Corps opened road communication with Florence via Highway 67. (*NARA*)

(**Above**) A Gurkha infantry section of the 10th Indian Division's 43rd Motorised Indian Infantry Brigade moves through a cleared path, indicated by white tape markers, in a ruined section of Faenza on 16 December 1944. Hitler had declared that Faenza was to be defended at all costs by the German 26th Panzer Division. The Gurkhas' next objective was to move north-west to positions along the Senio River, which they reached with two small bridgeheads the next day. (*NARA*)

(**Opposite, above**) Infantrymen and stretcher-bearers from the 2nd New Zealand Division move through rubble to cross a demolished bridge across the Lamone River into Faenza. After the Germans finally withdrew from Faenza on 22 December, Eighth Army sappers had to rebuild a bridge for Highway 9 across the Lamone River at Faenza in order to reach a new line on the eastern bank of the Senio River. (*NARA*)

(**Opposite, below**) Pack-laden infantrymen of the 2nd New Zealand Division move through Faenza in mid-December 1944. British V Corps had regrouped its divisions for the assault on the ancient city by 14 December, with the relatively fresh 10th Indian and 2nd New Zealand divisions moving into the bridgeheads across the Lamone River east of the Faenza. (*NARA*)

(**Opposite, above**) M4 medium tanks of the I Canadian Corps' 5th Armoured Division cross the Senio River on the Eighth Army's Adriatic coastal flank on 2 January 1945. After capturing Ravenna on 4 December 1944, the Canadians continued their northerly thrust, first crossing the Lamone River, and then eliminating two Nazi positions on the Senio River near Lake Comacchio's southern shore. (*NARA*)

(**Above**) In the Fifth Army's Northern Apennine sector, Company K of the US 91st Infantry Division's 361st Regiment leaves Loiano to fight for the village of Livergnano lying along Highway 65 amid the 10-mile-long Livergnano Escarpment, a steep east-west line of solitary mountain peaks, on 13 October 1944. The German Fourteenth Army's 4th Parachute, 65th Infantry and 362nd Infantry divisions were positioned there, constituting the Nazi's most strongly defended natural terrain position in the Northern Apennines. (*NARA*)

(**Opposite, below**) A Fifth Army supply truck deep in mud between Loiano and Livergnano, both situated on Highway 65 in the Northern Apennines, during US II Corps' 85th and 91st Infantry divisions' offensive against the Livergnano Escarpment during the first two weeks of October 1944. (*USAMHI*)

(**Opposite, above**) American troops push a Jeep bogged down in mud up a steep hill in the US II Corps sector's attack into the Northern Apennines northwards towards the Livergnano Escarpment on 11 October 1944. (*USAMHI*)

(**Opposite, below**) A Fifth Amy M4 medium tank and a Jeep ambulance both await orders to move out from the shelter of some partially destroyed buildings in the village of Livergnano on Highway 65 in mid-October 1944. In heavy combat, the US 85th Infantry Division took Monte delle Formiche on 10 October, while the 91st Division outflanked the Livergnano Escarpment from the west, forcing the Nazis to begin retreating from their positions beginning 13 October. (*NARA*)

(**Above**) A mortar team from the US 92nd Infantry ('Buffalo') Division in action near Massa on the US IV front in early October 1944. The American attack on the Ligurian coastal front was to give combat experience for Task Force 92, which consisted of the 92nd's 370th Infantry Regiment and the 2nd Armoured Group, the latter comprised the 434th and 435th Anti-aircraft (AA) battalions converted into infantry and supported by the 751st Tank Battalion and 849th Tank Destroyer Battalion. (*USAMHI*)

(**Opposite, above**) British XIII Corps infantrymen patrol through deep snow in their Northern Apennines sector as Fifth Army's right flank in late January 1945. On 27 October 1944, the Allied command ordered a halt to large-scale offensives. However, active patrolling and limited combat occurred during the winter's harsh conditions. (*NARA*)

(**Opposite, below**) American II Corps infantrymen from Company C, 1st Battalion of the veteran 34th Division's 135th Infantry Regiment patrol in winter camouflage uniforms near Tazzola in the vicinity of the Livergnano Escarpment on 25 January 1945. After the late October halt in major offensive operations, Keyes pulled back his II Corps troops southward to more defensible positions to prepare for the spring offensive. (*USAMHI*)

(**Above**) American infantrymen from the 10th Mountain Division trudge through snow carrying 75mm pack Howitzer ammunition to B Battery of the 616th Field Artillery Pack Battalion during the winter months of 1945. The 10th Mountain Division was part of US IV Corps and was situated between elements of the Brazilian Expeditionary Force on the left and the US 1st Armoured Division on their right. In January 1945, the Allies ceased any large-scale military operations, one factor being a limited artillery ammunition supply. (*NARA*)

(**Opposite, above**) A wounded soldier from the US 10th Mountain Division is evacuated by a medical litter team from the Monte Belvedere sector across snow-covered terrain. The 10th Mountain Division began arriving in Italy on 27 December 1944. Its mission was to eliminate enemy positions in the heights overlooking the US IV Corps sector prior to the spring offensive. The first phase of the 10th Mountain Division's mission began on 19 February 1945, against Monte Belvedere and Monte della Torraccia, which they captured from elements of the Nazi LI Mountain Corps, on 23 February. (*USAMHI*)

(**Above**) An M4 medium tank crew of the 6th South African Armoured Division loads 75mm shells into its armoured vehicle for the upcoming spring offensive against Bologna and the Po Valley. This armoured unit was part of US IV Corps and was situated along the Reno River east of Vergato in the Northern Apennines for the upcoming April 1945 attack. (*USAMHI*)

(**Opposite, below**) African-American infantrymen of Company C of the 92nd Division's 365th Regiment are pinned down by snipers while carrying ammunition in the vicinity of Monte Della Tessa on 10 January 1945. The 365th and 366th, unlike the 370th, were inexperienced in Italian combat conditions and action. In early February, the 92nd Division attacked enemy positions in the Serchio River Valley of IV Corps and made progress against the Italian fascist units there. However, the offensive stalled when they encountered veteran German formations. The 92nd suffered more than 700 casualties in four days of combat and pulled back to its original position. (*USAMHI*)

(**Above**) American infantrymen from Company B of the 85th Division's 339th Regiment march past a smoke canister to conceal their movement to relieve another unit in US II Corps sector of the Northern Apennines on 17 February 1945. Truscott, now commanding Fifth Army, attached the 339th and 337th regiments of the US 85th Division, along with the 2nd Brigade of British XIII Corps' 8th Indian Division, to the US IV Corps front on 23 December, where these units would be able to bolster the combat-inexperienced Allied forces on the Ligurian coast and in the Serchio River Valley. (*USAMHI*)

(**Opposite, above**) A platoon of American infantrymen from the 3rd Battalion of the 10th Mountain Division's 87th Regiment reaches one of its objectives and digs in on a ridgeline as part of the division's Operation Encore from 19 February–5 March 1945. Elements of the Brazilian Expeditionary Force were moving to the right of the 10th Mountain as US IV was advancing north-east towards Vergato on Highway 64, one of the two main roads along with Highway 65 that led to Bologna through the Northern Apennines. (*USAMHI*)

(**Opposite, below**) Infantrymen from the 10th Mountain Division fire a Browning 0.30-inch calibre light machine-gun at Nazi positions 200 yards away as they dig into a hilltop along Monte Della Vedetta as part of Operation Encore, which was to seize German-occupied heights situated above the Northern Apennines' mountain highways routes for the upcoming assault on Bologna in April 1945. (*USAMHI*)

(**Above**) A US 10th Mountain Division infantryman from Company K of the 87th Mountain Infantry Regiment covers a Nazi-occupied farmhouse 70 yards in the distance (*background*) with his Browning Automatic Rifle (BAR). Fifty-seven German soldiers were captured at this Monte Della Vedetta locale on 3 March 1945. (*USAMHI*)

(**Opposite, above**) American infantrymen from the 10th Mountain Division pass dead Nazi soldiers along the roadside in the Sassomolare area on 4 March 1945. The infantrymen are supported by M10 3-inch Gun Motor Carriages (GMC) of a tank destroyer battalion. (*USAMHI*)

(**Opposite, below**) An American infantry squad from the 1st Battalion of the 34th Division's 135th Regiment moves up a hill in the Northern Apennines on 6 March 1945. The squad carries a new, disassembled flat-trajectory two-man M18 shoulder-fired 57mm AT recoilless rifle. The M18 was almost entirely without recoil and had greater accuracy than the 57mm AT cannon. The weapon could be fired prone with a monopod or M1917A1 machine-gun tripod. The first of the M18 57mm AT guns were sent to Europe in March 1945 and subsequently sent to the Pacific for the Okinawa campaign. (*USAMHI*)

A British XIII Corps Royal Artillery gunner attached to the US Fifth Army ignites smoke canisters in the Northern Apennines to conceal Allied gun positions from Nazi observers in the heights to Imola's south-west near road No. 6528 in October 1944. *(NARA)*

British XIII Corps' 1st Division infantrymen attached to US Fifth Army advance up a steep incline towards Monte Pratone, north of the pierced Gothic Line, in late September 1944. The ultimate target of the British 1st Division was Monte Battaglia in the Northern Apennines situated to Imola's south-west. *(NARA)*

An M7 'Priest' 105mm Gun Motor Carriage (GMC) of the British 1st Division's 1st Guards Brigade in the muddy centre of a Northern Apennine Italian village. This British XIII Corps unit, attached to the US Fifth Army, was to relieve the US 88th Division on 5 October 1944 after the Americans seized Monte Battaglia as one arm of Clark's forces advanced along Route 6528 towards Imola on Highway 9. (*NARA*)

Chapter Seven

Po Valley to the Alps and Victory in Italy

The Allied spring offensive was the plan for Eighth Army to attack westward into the area between the Senio and Reno rivers while Fifth Army advanced northwards to the west of Bologna. However, the Germans flooded large areas of ground on both sides of the Reno River to the west of Lake Comacchio. Highway 16 from Ravenna to Ferrara was the only firm ground for armour, notably at the village of Argenta near the junction of the Reno, Idice and Sillaro rivers – the 'Argenta Gap'. It was Alexander's intent to trap the German armies between the two Allied ones. The launch of this spring offensive into the Po Valley was 9 April 1945.

Eighth Army's British V Corps was to attack over the Senio on a wide front aiming towards the Argenta Gap. The Polish II Corps, with many of its soldiers and commanders disheartened by the political manoeuvring between Stalin and Roosevelt at Yalta to place Poland under Soviet hegemony, was also to attack over the Senio to the north of Highway 9, which led to Imola and then Bologna.

Along the Ligurian coast, on 5 April, the combat-bloodied and reconstituted US 92nd ('Buffalo') Infantry Division, with the recently returned Japanese-American *Nisei* 442nd RCT, the US 473rd Infantry regiments and other *ad hoc* units were to mount a diversionary raid on the coast. On 11–12 April, IV Corps' US 1st Armoured and 10th Mountain divisions, along with the Brazilian Expeditionary Force, were supposed to attack towards Bazzano, 10 miles west of Bologna. Then IV Corps units were to sever Highway 9 to Bologna's west and dispatch the US 1st Armoured and US II Corps' 6th South African Armoured divisions towards the Po River crossings near Ostiglia and north of Bondeno. Keyes' US II Corps' 34th, 85th, 88th and 91st Infantry divisions, situated on the east side of Reno River to the north of the mountain passes, were slated to directly attack Bologna from both sides commencing on 12 April.

The Eighth Army's preliminary attacks occurred on 1 April, as British Commandos and infantry from the 24th Guards Brigade seized a portion of Lake Comacchio on the Adriatic coast to the north of the British V Corps' 56th Division's front. Four days later, some islands in the lake were seized and, on 6 April, the 56th Division crossed the Reno and captured ground leading up the lake's shores.

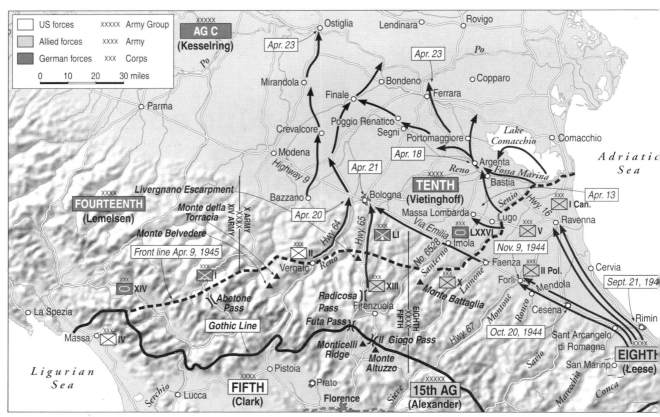

Into the Po Valley: The Northern Apennines and the Romagna Plain. Eighth Army, throughout the autumn and early winter, crossed successive defended river lines along the flooded Romagna Plain, the Savio, Ronco, Montone, Lamone and Senio, to advance along the Highway 9 corridor. Cesena and Forli were seized on 20 October and 9 November 1944, respectively, followed by Faenza's capture in mid-December. Eighth Army halted along the Senio River line for the winter until drier weather enabled an offensive toward the Argenta Gap and the Po River. In Fifth Army's Northern Apennine sector, the centre US II Corps, with British XIII on the right and US IV Corps on the left, came within 10 miles of Bologna during tough winter mountain campaigning waged along rivers and Highways 64, 65 and 67, and secondary roads such as No. 6528. Allied supply, ammunition, and manpower shortages mandated Fifth Army return to defensible positions to await a spring offensive.

Eighth Army's preliminary attacks commenced on 1 April 1945 at Lake Comacchio. On 6 April, British V Corps' 56th Division crossed the Reno to the lake's southern shore. On 9 April, 8th Indian and 2nd New Zealand divisions attacked across the Senio River's high flood banks on either side of Lugo. On 11 April, Gurkhas and Royal Fusiliers crossed the Santerno River while Massa Lombardo was attacked on 13 April. The Reno River at Bastia was crossed by the 78th Division on 14 April. On 16 April, the British 78th and 56th Infantry divisions crossed the 12-foot Fossa Marina Canal, west of Lake Comacchio. The next day both divisions, with 2nd Armoured Brigade tanks, moved on Argenta, which was cleared on 18 April. Dry terrain towards Ferrara and the Po River awaited Eighth Army.

On 15 April, US II Corps divisions moved up Highway 65 towards Bologna. On 20 April, the US IV Corps' 10th Mountain divisions reached Highway 9 between Bologna and Modena as the II Corps' 85th Division reached Highway 65 just east of the city. Bologna was captured by American and Polish troops on 21 April. The 6th South African Armoured Division, having crossed to the western side of the Reno River, traversed Highway 9 and advanced north into the Po Valley towards Finale and the Po River. (*Philip Schwartzberg, Meridian Mapping*)

On 9 April, the British V Corps' 8th Indian and 2nd New Zealand divisions attacked across the Senio River's high flood banks, using bulldozers and Churchill two-tiered Armoured Ramp Carrier (ARK) tanks, on either side of the town of Lugo. Their ultimate task was to seize a bridgehead across the Santerno River, which the Indian and British infantrymen of the 8th Indian Division reached by the next evening. On 11 April, after massive aerial and artillery bombardment, Gurkhas and Royal Fusiliers crossed the Santerno, and the British 78th Infantry Division moved through the 8th Indian Division's infantry to commence its attack on Bastia, with the ultimate target being the town of Argenta on Highway 16 and access to manoeuvrable terrain within the Po Valley. The bridge over the Reno River at Bastia was crossed by the 78th Division on the morning of 14 April. The New Zealanders, to the left of the 8th Indian and now British 78th Infantry divisions, also successfully crossed the two rivers and moved onto Massa Lombarda by 13 April. The Polish II Corps crossed the Senio and Santerno rivers to advance on Imola, east of Bologna on Highway 9. The Polish advance was a vital element for the US Fifth Army's assault from the south of the city. During these Eighth Army attacks, the different Allied corps also faced the German Tenth Army's 26th Panzer, 98th and 362nd Infantry, 4th Parachute and 42nd Jaeger divisions across the entire front, gradually pushing them north towards the vital Argenta Gap just west of the impassable Lake Comacchio.

On 16 April, a full-scale attack by the British 78th and 56th Infantry divisions was launched across the Fossa Marina, a 12-foot canal running south-west from Lake Comacchio to Argenta. By the afternoon of 17 April, elements of both infantry divisions, along with the British 2nd Armoured Brigade, began moving through the area north of the Fossa Marina. Argenta was finally cleared by the British 78th Infantry Division on 18 April and McCreery released the British 6th Armoured Division from his reserve to advance on a north-westward axis of Argenta-Segni-Poggio Renatico-;Finale. The British armoured brigades advanced through thickly wooded country, as roads were avoided because of landmines, and threatened to outflank the entire Nazi Tenth Army front.

US Fifth Army's main attack commenced during the morning of 14 April after a two-day postponement from bad weather to allow for a massive preparatory Allied aerial bombardment. In the IV Corps sector, the US 1st Armoured and 10th Mountain divisions, along with the Brazilians, attacked on the western side of the Reno River. After two days of stubborn German resistance mounted by the Nazi Fourteenth Army's 94th Infantry and 90th Panzer Grenadier divisions of the XIV Panzer Corps, Truscott's units progressed about 6 miles and began to detect faltering enemy defences in the Northern Apennines.

On 15 April, along the US II Corps front, Keyes' divisions moved up Highway 65 towards Bologna, following an Allied heavy bomber raid that concentrated on the areas between Highways 64 and 65 and the defences around Bologna. US II Corps faced the German 65th Infantry and 8th Mountain divisions of the XIV Panzer Corps and the 1st Parachute and 305th Infantry divisions of the I Parachute Corps. The 6th South African Armoured Division, on the eastern side of the Reno River, and the US 88th Infantry Division opened up the II Corps offensive moving towards objectives between the paralleling Highways 64 and 65. The US II Corps' 34th, 88th, and 91st Infantry divisions advanced up the Highway 65 corridor towards Bologna, attacking heavily defended Nazi hill positions over the next two days. On 17 April, Truscott released the US 85th Infantry Division from Fifth Army reserve to Keyes' II Corps for a final push up Highway 65.

On 20 April, the US IV Corps' 10th Mountain divisions reached Highway 9 between Bologna and Modena. Also, US II Corps' 85th Division reached Highway 65 just to the east of Bologna. The 6th South African Armoured Division, having crossed to the western side of the Reno River, now traversed Highway 9 as well and advanced north into the flat terrain of the Po Valley towards Finale and the Po River, 30 miles to the north. Fifth Army emerged from the Northern Apennines after months of deadlocked combat.

With Allied tanks converging on the German Tenth Army from the both the Bologna and Argenta areas, Vietinghoff ordered his forces to withdraw to the line of the Po River on 20 April. Two days later, the British and South African 6th Armoured divisions reached Finale to the north-west of the Reno River. The Polish II Corps, moving west along Highway 9, and the US II Corps' 34th Division, advancing north up Highway 65, entered Bologna on 21 April. It was a fitting entrance for these veteran units of the different Cassino battles. The US 10th Mountain Division reached the Po River opposite Ostiglia on 22 April after advancing 55 miles in a few days. The Eighth Army's 8th Indian Division was in Ferrara south of the river a day later. The flat terrain and excellent road network in the Po Valley enabled the Fifth and Eighth armies to conduct rapid armoured thrusts from the Apennine foothills towards the Po River and the Alpine foothills beyond. Due to the speed of the Allied advances, more than 100,000 German troops were forced to surrender south of the Po River. By 24 April, the entire Fifth Army front was on the Po River.

The Germans left nearly all of their artillery, tanks and transport at ferry locales on the south bank of the Po River, much of it having been destroyed by Allied air superiority. After crossing the Po River, the US 10th Mountain Division was one of the three American divisions that helped capture Verona on 25–26 April. The British 6th Armoured Division's armoured cars and other reconnaissance vehicles crossed the Po on 24 April with the 2nd New Zealand and British 56th divisions also establishing bridgeheads that day.

To the north of the Po River was the Adige River, with its destroyed bridges, flowing north through Verona and east into the Gulf of Venice. However, the rapidity of the Allied advance prevented the Germans, now depleted of ordnance, from fully

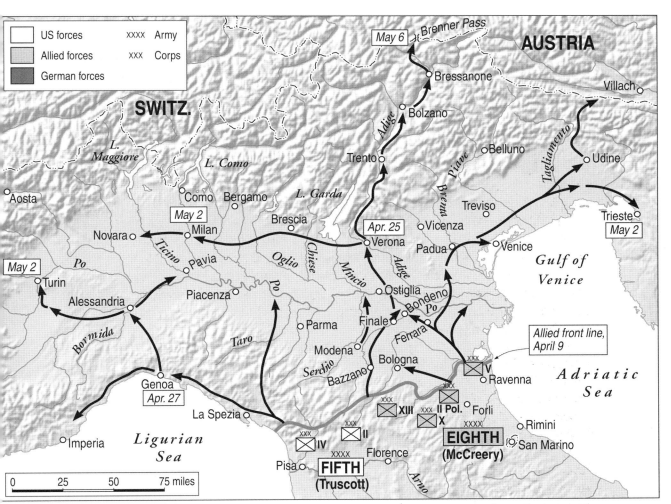

Across the Po River to the Alps. The US 10th Mountain Division reached the Po River opposite Ostiglia on 22 April 1945. The Eighth Army's 8th Indian Division was in Ferrara a day later. Flat terrain and excellent road networks enabled the Fifth and Eighth armies to conduct rapid armoured thrusts from the Northern Apennine foothills towards the Po River and the Alpine foothills beyond. By 24 April, the entire Fifth Army front was on the Po River. The British 6th Armoured Division's armoured cars and other reconnaissance vehicles crossed the Po on 24 April, with the 2nd New Zealand and British 56th divisions also establishing bridgeheads that day. US 10th Mountain Division was one of the three American divisions that helped capture Verona on 25 – 26 April. British, New Zealand and US 91st Infantry divisions began crossing the Adige River to the east on 25 April. The US 88th Infantry Division, after crossing the Adige on 26 April, moved onto Vicenza. The US 10th Mountain and 1st Armoured divisions moved north to seal the Brenner Pass and other possible German escape routes into Austria and Switzerland. The US 92nd Infantry Division entered Genoa on 27 April. Milan was captured on 2 May, as was Turin. New Zealand troops and Yugoslavian communist partisans reached Trieste on 3 May, with German forces surrendering to the Allies in fear of civilian reprisals. (*Philip Schwartzberg, Meridian Mapping*)

manning the Adige Line of trenches and dug-outs in the Alpine foothills. British, New Zealand and US 91st Infantry divisions began crossing the Adige River on 25 April against weak resistance. The US II Corps' 88th Infantry Division crossed the Adige at Verona on 26 April and prepared to move north-east on Vicenza 25 miles away. Now American units such as the 10th Mountain and 1st Armoured divisions were tasked with moving quickly to seal the Brenner Pass and other possible German escape routes into Austria and Switzerland.

Under attack by local Italian partisans, German units started to surrender without a direct order. At the port city of Genoa, the US 92nd Infantry Division entered the city on 27 April without any resistance as the 4,000-man German garrison surrendered to Italian partisans the day before. On 29 April, two German officers representing General Vietinghoff and Lieutenant-General Karl Wolff, the supreme SS commander in Italy, signed an unconditional surrender at 15th Army Group headquarters in Caserta of the remaining German forces south of the Alps. With Nazi communications severely compromised, the Allies agreed to a three-day interval for notification of the scattered enemy units, resulting in the massive German capitulation in Italy and Austria becoming effective on 2 May 1945. The Italian campaign ended almost two years after the Allied invasion of Sicily's south-eastern shores on 10 July 1943.

(**Opposite, above**) British Eighth Army's 24th Guards Brigade infantrymen cross a flooded plain along the eastern side of Lake Comacchio north of Ravenna on the Adriatic coast in April 1945. These infantrymen joined No. 10 British Commandos in the operation to outflank German defences guarding Highway 16 to facilitate the Eighth Army's entry into the Po Valley towards Ferrara and the Po River crossings. (*NARA*)

(**Opposite, below**) No. 10 British Commandos of the 2nd Commando Brigade march along a dyke onto the flooded plain near the Argenta Gap on 1–2 April 1945, after crossing from the south-eastern corner of Lake Comacchio and capturing some mid-lake islands. Other 2nd Commando Brigade units involved in Operation Roast were No. 9 British Commandos, No. 43 Royal Marine (RM) Commandos and the Special Raiding Squadron. The German defences along the wide but shallow Lake Comacchio were to impede Eighth Army's progress through the Argenta Gap, between the lake and the Reno River, into the Po Valley. However, many Allied amphibious vehicles became bogged down in the lake's shallow water and deep mud. West of the lake, the Senio, Santerno and Idice rivers – all tributaries of the meandering Reno River – were Nazi river defence lines to bar Eighth Army's north-westward advance to Bologna and the Po River. Along the Argenta Gap, the German LXXVI Panzer Corps had twelve incomplete divisions with Mk VI Panzers, self-propelled 88mm guns and assorted other artillery pieces awaiting the Eighth Army move. The 2nd Commando Brigade required three days to cross Lake Comacchio before joining the British 56th Infantry Division for the assault on the Argenta Gap. (*NARA*)

(**Opposite**) A British XIII Corps motorised column moves along a narrow road through the Northern Apennines in early April 1945. On 18 January 1945, XIII Corps, commanded by Alexander's former chief of staff, Lieutenant-General John Harding, comprised the left wing of the Eighth Army. McCreery waited for dry weather before crossing the numerous rivers no longer in flood stage on the Romagna Plain. (*NARA*)

(**Above**) A 2nd New Zealand Division Jeep convoy moves through Granarola towards Massa Lombarda on 13 April 1945, during its westward advance across the Senio and Santerno rivers on the Romagna Plain paralleling Highway 9 between Faenza and Imola. On 9–10 April, the New Zealanders in the centre, along with the 8th Indian Division's 19th Brigade on the right and elements of the II Polish Corps on the left, moved across the Senio River as part of Eighth Army's set-piece battle, Operation Grapeshot, against the German 98th and 362nd Infantry divisions. The combined arms attack incorporated armour, infantry, artillery and a heavy and medium bomber assault, with more than 800 planes, using fragmentation bombs to avoid cratering. Eighth Army crossed the Santerno River and captured Massa Lombarda on 13 April. (*NARA*)

(**Opposite, above**) A Churchill Crocodile flame-throwing tank during Operation Grapeshot's attack across the Senio River on 12 April 1945. This particular armoured vehicle, named Calgary, accompanied New Zealand infantry and was instrumental at reducing enemy bunkers with flame and gunfire from its 6-pounder turret gun. (*NARA*)

(**Opposite, below**) Churchill Infantry tanks of the British 6th Armoured Division move across some of the undulating drier ground in the drive towards the Argenta Gap in mid- April 1945. Often the armour moved cross-country in a deliberate attempt to avoid German Tenth Army-mined local roads. (*NARA*)

(**Above**) Infantrymen of the British 56th Division, as part of V Corps, attend to a fellow soldier wounded by a German rifle grenade along a village's roadside in the drive towards Argenta. After absorbing the British 2nd Commando Brigade into its formation, the 56th crossed the Reno River on 5–6 April 1945 at the southern end of Lake Comacchio. (*NARA*)

A British 78th Division infantry section moves cautiously amid the rubble of Argenta. The Battle for the Argenta Gap commenced on 10–11 April 1945. The 78th Division, which bridged the Reno River at Bastia situated along Highway 16 on 14 April, met fierce resistance from the German 29th Panzer Grenadier Division defending Argenta. The battle continued for four days drawing other V Corps units into the fray. (*Author's Collection*)

New Zealand 2nd Division infantrymen move wooden assault boats into position atop a steep floodbank to cross the Senio River near Lugo. After crossing the river on 12–13 April, the next target for the New Zealanders was Massa Lombarda near the Santerno River, which was reached on 14 April, driving the Nazis across the next river line, the Sillaro. (*Author's Collection*)

An Allied Sexton 25-pounder Self-Propelled Gun crosses the formidable floodbank of the shallow Senio River in mid-April 1945. This Sexton utilised two Churchill Armoured Ramp Carrier (ARK) tanks as the span between the steep banks of the river. The ARK was a turretless Churchill Infantry tank with a plate welded over the space with wooden tracks across the top. The ARK traversed ditches or obstacles as its folding ramps were lowered to form the bridge. The Sexton used a Canadian Ram tank chassis and housed the veritable 25-pounder along with two Bren light machine-guns and one 0.5-inch calibre Browning AA machine-gun. (*Author's Collection*)

(**Above**) After crossing the Senio River, the 2nd New Zealand Division approached the Santerno River after capturing Lugo on 12–13 April 1945. Lugo was in the middle of an east-west axis of Ravenna on the Adriatic coast and Bologna, a main Allied 15th Army Group target of the spring offensive. (*NARA*)

(**Opposite, above**) A British 78th Division Bren gunner near a Senio River crossing to the north-east of Lugo in mid-April 1945. After crossing the Senio, the 78th traversed the Santerno and then the Reno River at Bastia along Highway 16 to assist the British 56th Division's attack on Argenta, taken on 18 April. The way towards Ferrara, the Po Valley, and ultimately the Po River crossings, was open. (*NARA*)

(**Opposite, below**) US M8 75mm Howitzer Gun Motor Carriages of the African-American 758th Tank Battalion fire uphill into the mountains from behind a stone wall in Seravezza along the Ligurian coast in April 1945. This armoured battalion was an attached unit supporting the US 442nd (*Nisei*) RCT's advance to outflank Massa from the east. By late March 1945, the 442nd returned to Italy and was amalgamated with the 92nd ('Buffalo') Division's battle-hardened 370th Infantry Regiment. On 5 April, the 370th, along with the 442nd, began its diversionary attack up the Ligurian coastal highway toward Massa. However, heavy Nazi artillery fire halted them. (*NARA*)

Medics from the US 92nd Division's 370th Infantry Regiment rescue survivors of a mortar attack on the 100th Battalion of the 442nd (*Nisei*) RCT. Six of the Japanese-American soldiers were killed by the blasts near Seravezza in April 1945 as part of these regiments' advance on Massa up the Ligurian coast. (*USAMHI*)

(**Opposite, below**) Two mountain infantrymen of the US 10th Mountain Division with their pack mule observe some of their division ride an M4 medium tank in the Northern Apennines in April 1945. This elite division began arriving in Italy in late December 1944. Through late February–early March 1945, the division's three mountain infantry regiments were engaged in the right wing of IV Corps' Operation Encore to seize a solid line of ridges and mountain crests for the upcoming Allied spring offensive onto Bologna and into the Po Valley. (*USAMHI*)

(**Above**) D Troop of the 81st Cavalry Reconnaissance Squadron of the US 1st Armoured Division prepares to leave the battered town of Vergato on 15 April 1945 in a Jeep column. Vergato, situated on Highway 64, was on the US IV Corps' 1st Armoured Division axis of advance. The 81st Cavalry Reconnaissance Squadron began the Fifth Army's spring offensive on 12 April by storming into heavily defended Vergato, but was halted by enemy mortar and machine-gunfire that necessitated a brutal house-to-house reduction of this picturesque Northern Apennine locale. The US 10th Mountain Division was on the left flank of the armour near Highway 64, which ran north into the south-western end of Bologna situated along Highway 9. (*NARA*)

(**Above**) German soldiers of the 297th Alpine (*Gebirgsjäger*) Regiment of the Nazi 8th Mountain (*Gebirgs*) Division surrender to elements of the US II Corps' 88th Infantry Division on 16–18 April 1945. The action took place in the Monte Rumici area, which was located east of Highway 64 and the Reno River between Montes Sole and Adone to the south of Bologna. (*NARA*)

(**Opposite, above**) Infantrymen of the US 88th Division examine large amounts of Nazi ordnance captured on 18 April in some caves of Monte Rumici to the south of Monte Adone. Elements of the 88th Division moved through this Northern Apennines sector defended by the German 65th Infantry Division between the Reno and Savena rivers, each of which paralleled Highways 64 and 65, respectively. (*NARA*)

(**Opposite, below**) A 155mm Howitzer of the US 10th Mountain Division fires on enemy positions in the Campidello area near Monte Pastore astride the Lavino River, a small river in the Emilia-Romagna region, 11 miles to Bologna's south-west, on 20 April 1945. (*NARA*)

(**Above**) The 3rd Platoon, Company G, 86th Mountain Infantry Regiment of the US 10th Mountain Division advances along a narrow road towards the next ridge beyond Monte Valbura on 14 April 1945. The 10th Mountain and US 1st Armoured divisions moved abreast through the Panaro and Reno river valleys. Each division staggered their attack to allow for concentrated American artillery fire on the next target. Control of successive ridgelines and mountain crests by the 10th Mountain Division eased the advance of the 1st Armoured Division and demonstrated the need for close tank-infantry co-operation in this terrain. Both divisions were ultimately tasked with the seizure of Ponte Samoggia, a village to Bologna's north-west on Highway 9, to gain entry into the Po Valley for a rapid thrust towards the Po River. (*USAMHI*)

(**Opposite, above**) Infantrymen from Company A of the US 88th Division's 350th Regiment cover sappers of the 6th South African Armoured Division with a 0.30-inch calibre machine-gun on 19 April 1945. The South Africans cleared landmines sown by the retreating German 8th Mountain (*Gebirgs*) Division on a small road west of Highway 64 and the Reno River. (*NARA*)

(**Opposite, below**) Elements of the US 91st Infantry Division move up a road through the Northern Apennines' foothills, near Casalecchio, to Bologna's south-west, with M4 medium tanks of the 6th South African Armoured Division. This force confronted the Nazi 8th Mountain (*Gebirgs*) Division on 20–21 April 1945. Both Highway 64 and the Reno River run through Casalecchio. (*NARA*)

(**Opposite, above**) American infantrymen pass German road signs indicating the direction and distance to Bologna along Highway 9. As is evident, the surrounding terrain consisted of mountain crests and intervening valleys with patches of farmland. (*NARA*)

(**Above**) An M4 medium tank of the British Eighth Army's II Polish Corps rolls down a Bolognese street on 21 April 1945, coincident with the entry of the US II Corps' 34th Division that day. The Eighth Army had been moving from the east, principally with the Poles, along Highway 9 from Imola. (*NARA*)

(**Opposite, below**) An American half-track of the US 34th Infantry Division returns fire against German snipers in Bologna on 21 April 1945. The return fire consists of a 0.50-inch calibre AA machine-gun mounted on the half-track along with an infantryman firing his 0.45-inch calibre Thompson submachine-gun. (*NARA*)

(**Above**) An M4 medium tank of the US 1st Armoured Division moves through the Piazza Duomo of Bologna after the city fell to Allied forces on 21 April 1945. By dawn of 22 April, the entire Fifth Army was well into the Po Valley, while elements of the Eighth Army, after moving through the Argenta Gap on 18 April, were swarming across the valley towards Ferrara, Finale and the Po River crossings. Elements of the Nazis' 1st and 4th Parachute divisions had put up forlorn rear-guard resistance beyond Bologna and elsewhere attempting to delay the Allied advance so that small detachments of the German Tenth Army could retreat across the Po River. Nonetheless, tens of thousands of Germans were captured in the Allied advance toward the river crossings. (*NARA*)

(**Opposite, above**) A German motorised convoy in ruins after Allied fighter-bomber attacks on the southern bank of the Po River at Felonica, a ferry service point, on 25 April 1945. Allied air power had previously destroyed all of the bridges across the Po. Over 100,000 Germans were forced to surrender in the areas south of the Po River during the last week of April. (*NARA*)

(**Opposite, below**) Infantrymen of the US 10th Mountain Division form a bridgehead on the northern bank of the Po River after being ferried across by amphibious vehicles. By 24 April, the entire Fifth Army front arrived along the southern bank of the Po River. German artillery, firing air bursts, failed to deter the river crossing, although there were some casualties. By the late afternoon of that day, two of the division's mountain infantry regiments were across the Po with the third to be ferried across overnight. (*NARA*)

(**Opposite, above**) At Ostiglia, half-track quadruple-mounted 0.50-inch calibre machine-guns of the 432nd AA Artillery Battalion attached to the 88th Division's 351st Infantry Regiment provide covering fire for the Po River crossings on 24 April 1945. Elements of the US 10th Mountain Division also crossed in this sector. (*NARA*)

(**Above**) An American 57mm AT gun along the southern bank of the Po River at Ostiglia situated near a touring car. The gun crew is firing the weapon at enemy positions along the northern bank on 24 April 1945. British Eighth Army units were also closing in on the southern river bank the day before, including the British 6th Armoured Division north of Bondeno, the 8th Indian Division north of Ferrara and the British 56th Division further to the east. (*NARA*)

(**Opposite, below**) A US 88th Infantry Division headquarters officer observes the Po River crossing with amphibious vehicles through binoculars while standing on the rear of his Jeep, on 24 April 1945. The dust on the uniforms and vehicles attested the rapid transit of Allied units across the Po Valley during the last ten days of April. (*NARA*)

(**Above**) M5 light tanks of the 91st Cavalry Reconnaissance Squadron of the US 1st Armoured Division emerge through a bulldozed portion of the southern floodbank of the Po River and onto an M-2 treadway pontoon bridge for the waterway's crossing to the far shore on 25 April 1945. The temporary bridge had been quickly assembled by the US 401st Engineer Battalion. (*NARA*)

(**Opposite, above**) US 88th Division infantrymen in two Amtracs cross the Po River, with a destroyed bridge's span in the far background. This amphibious vehicle's 0.50-inch calibre machine-guns are enclosed in armoured protective mounts. The 88th crossed the Po at two sites against patchy enemy resistance, as evidenced by this photograph. (*NARA*)

(**Opposite, below**) An infantry column of the US 10th Mountain Division's 87th Regiment's 3rd Battalion marches up both sides of a road in single file north of the Po River. From 24–26 April 1945, the Fifth Army advances from the Po River bridgeheads effectively divided Nazi forces in northern Italy. The 10th Mountain Division began their speedy advance north of the river early on 25 April, and by morning had moved to within 20 miles of Verona. The US II Corps' 85th and 88th Infantry divisions also pushed to the outskirts of Verona within a twenty-four-hour period after crossing the Po. (*USAMHI*)

(**Above**) A column of infantrymen from the US 85th Division marches past German corpses lying along a Verona street, which fell to the US II Corps' divisions and the 10th Mountain Division on 26 April 1945. Elements of the US 88th Division secured the town after tense combat the night before, with the 85th and 10th divisions moving in soon thereafter. The seizure of Verona brought the Fifth Army up to the final Nazi defensive line in northern Italy, the Adige Line. (*NARA*)

(**Opposite, above**) M5 light tanks of the 91st Cavalry Reconnaissance Squadron of the US 1st Armoured Division move through the wrecked Verona railway station on 26 April 1945. In contrast to this armoured column, the American infantry divisions had raced 40 miles from the Po River crossings to the outskirts of Verona in an array of commandeered vehicles. (*NARA*)

(**Opposite, below**) Infantrymen of the US 91st Division's 362nd Regiment cross the Adige River at the town of Legnano, to Verona's south-east across a makeshift wood plank surface to the side of the demolished steel bridge and concrete abutments. After crossing the Po River, the 91st advanced on a north-eastward axis with the 6th South African Armoured Division on its right towards Legnano. The lack of manpower and ordnance, as well as the speed of the Allied advance through the Po Valley and north of the Po River, had prevented the Nazis from organising a meaningful Adige Line defence amid the network of trenches, dug-outs and pillboxes. (*USAMHI*)

Company I of the US 34th Infantry Division's 135th Regiment, veterans of North Africa, Cassino and Anzio, move down a Parma street lined with citizens, on 26 April 1945. After emerging from the Northern Apennines into the Po Valley, the 34th pushed along Highway 9 to Parma. After Parma, the 34th moved 50 miles north-west on Highway 9 to Piacenza, just south of the Po River, which was captured on 28 April. (NARA)

Tank crewmen attached to the US 88th Division carry a wounded soldier in Vicenza to Verona's north-east and just south of the Alps, on 28 April 1945. The 88th Division left the Adige River for Vicenza and arrived on 28 April, clearing the city in house-to-house combat. Thousands of Nazis were captured in the process of blocking any remaining escape routes to the north. (NARA)

An infantryman from the US 88th Division runs through a street in Vicenza past two Nazi-demolished trucks, on 28 April 1945. The 88th Division, after mopping up operations in Vicenza, moved north-eastward towards the Piave River north of Treviso to effect a rendezvous with the US Seventh Army moving south from Austria, which occurred on 4 May. (NARA)

Epilogue

The Italian campaign at its peak involved almost 500,000 Allied combatants. From Sicily to south of the Alps, from July 1943 to May 1945, the Allied armies had fought in horrific terrain and under miserable weather conditions during their 1,000 miles of advancing combat. At the time of the signing of the unconditional surrender of German forces in Italy, the US Fifth Army had been in continuous combat for 600 days since Salerno. During the Italian campaign, more than 310,000 Allied casualties were incurred with 190,000 sustained by Fifth Army units.

The British Eighth Army had marched more than 3,000 miles since El Alamein in November 1942. During the Italian campaign's combat operations, from 3 September 1943 until 2 May 1945, the Eighth Army suffered just over 123,000 casualties.

Of the almost 32,000 Allied soldiers killed, approximately 20,000 were Americans with the remainder being British and Commonwealth troops, Frenchmen, Poles, Brazilians, members of the Jewish Brigade and liberated Italian battle groups. German losses in Italy have been estimated to have exceeded 430,000 total casualties with 48,000 killed in action and more than 214,000 missing. The Italian countryside, unfortunately, became dotted with too many combatant graveyards and cemeteries.

At Churchill's urging, the new American president upon Roosevelt's death, Harry S. Truman, acceded to the British prime minister's desire to capture Trieste on the Adriatic Sea's eastern shore and the province of Venezia Giulia. Elements of Eighth Army's 2nd New Zealand Division raced 80 miles from the Piave River with their orders to seize Trieste before Tito's partisans could occupy the city. Both the New Zealanders and the Yugoslav partisans met at Monfalcone during the late hours of 1 May, and both forces occupied Trieste on 3 May. The Germans surrendered to Freyberg's troops, fearing reprisals from the communist guerrillas. The New Zealanders' presence, and then American and British servicemen, ultimately allowed the province of Venezia Giulia to remain Italian. The seeds of the 'Cold War' were immediately being sown at the end of the Second World War.

It remains to be argued if the Italian campaign fulfilled Churchill's desire to ascend the 'soft underbelly' of the mountainous peninsula to get to Vienna and the Balkans before the Soviets. In fact, Churchill had written to Field Marshal Jan Smuts of South Africa as early as December 1944:

> If the powers of evil prevail in Greece, as is quite likely, we must be prepared for a quasi-Bolshevised Balkans peninsula, and this may spread to Italy and Hungary. I therefore see great perils to the world in these quarters.

Other military analysts and former commanders have contended that it was an Allied 'holding operation' to pin down Nazi formations that may have defended the Russian and north-west Europe fronts, the latter after the successful Normandy invasion. Intriguingly, Kesselring believed that his Army Group C tied down hundreds of thousands of Allied troops, along with a myriad armoured vehicles and artillery pieces. The debate will rage about the campaign's ultimate goals. However, neither the casualties incurred nor the combatants' valour exhibited can be forgotten.

General Mark Clark, commanding general of the Allied 15th Army Group, hands over documents of surrender to German General Fridolin von Senger und Etterlin, the representative of General Heinrich von Vietinghoff, the Nazi Army Group C commander. This ceremony occurred during the afternoon of 3 May 1945 at Allied 15th Army Group headquarters in Caserta. General Richard McCreery (*right*), the British Eighth Army commanding general, and Lieutenant-General Lucian Truscott (*not shown*), who led the US Fifth Army since December 1944, were also in attendance. The evening before, Clark's headquarters transmitted the cease-fire throughout northern Italy as German forces laid down their weapons. (*USAMHI*)

The beaten corpses of Benito Mussolini and his mistress, Claretta Petacci, are propped up by Italian partisans for public display. On 28 April 1945, partisans had found and executed Mussolini and Petacci at his Gargnano villa near Lake Como. Their bodies were moved to Milan, the largest city in northern Italy, where they were strung up by their heels on the Piazzale Loreto. Milan had been liberated by the partisans before the US 1st Armoured Division arrived on 30 April. However, local Italians had exacted their revenge on the former *Duce* and subjected him to a brutal, ignoble end. *(NARA)*

American infantrymen from the US 88th Division and a column of M4 medium tanks of the US 752nd Tank Battalion pass the corpse of a German soldier lying on a sidewalk in the town of Cornuda on 28 April 1945 in the Italian province of Treviso. Other Allied formations, such as the US 91st Infantry and British 6th Armoured divisions, also arrived in the vicinity. At this time, both German and pro-fascist Italians were being hunted by Italian partisans who wanted revenge. (*USAMHI*)

A German military policeman and his American counterpart from the US 85th Infantry Division directing traffic through the Brenner Pass to Austria after hostilities formally ended on 3 May 1945. On 2 May, elements of the British Eighth Army reached Trieste along the eastern shore of the Adriatic Sea to unite with communist partisans under Marshal Josip Broz Tito of Yugoslavia. (NARA)

References

Atkinson, R. (2007), *The Day of Battle. The War in Sicily and Italy, 1943–1944* (Holt Paperbacks, New York).

Blumenson, M. (2001), *Anzio. The Gamble that Failed* (Cooper Square Press, New York).

Brooks, T. (2001), *The War North of Rome: June 1944–May 1945*. (Castle Books, Edison).

Carver, M. (2002), *The Imperial War Museum Book of the War in Italy 1943–1945* (Pan Books, London).

Clark, L. (2006), *Anzio. Italy and the Battle for Rome – 1944* (Headline Review, London).

D'Este, C. (1991), *Fatal Decision. Anzio and the Battle for Rome* (Harper Collins, New York).

D'Este, C. (1990), *World War II in the Mediterranean 1942–1945* (Algonquin Books, Chapel Hill).

Diamond, J. (2017), *First Blood in North Africa. Operation Torch and the U.S. Campaign in Africa in World War II* (Stackpole Books, Guilford).

Diamond, J. (2017), *The Invasion of Sicily 1943* (Pen & Sword, Barnsley).

Diamond, J. (2018), *The Invasion of the Italian Mainland: Salerno to the Gustav Line 1943–1944* (Pen & Sword, Barnsley).

Fisher, E.F., Jr. (1993), *The Mediterranean Theater of Operations: Cassino to the Alps* (US Government Printing Office, Washington, DC).

Graham, D. and Bidwell, S. (1986), *Tug of War* (St Martin's Press, New York).

Harpur, B. (1980), *The Impossible Victory. A Personal Account of the Battle for the River Po* (Hippocrene Books, New York).

Neillands, R. (2004), *Eighth Army: The Triumphant Desert Army That Held the Axis at Bay from North Africa to the Alps, 1939–45* (Overlook Press, Woodstock).

Orgill, D. (1967), *The Gothic Line. The Italian Campaign, Autumn 1944* (Curtis Books, New York).

Perret, G. (1991), *There's A War to be Won. The United States Army in World War II* (Ballentine Books, New York).

Porch, D. (2004), *The Path to Victory. The Mediterranean Theater in World War II* (Farrar, Straus and Giroux, New York).

Tucker-Jones, A. (2013), *Armoured Warfare in the Italian Campaign 1943–1945* (Pen & Sword, Barnsley).

Notes

Notes

Notes

Notes

Notes